THE INDIAN DEMOCRACY AND THE COMMON MAN

PRO-POOR, GENDER-EQUITY AND ECO-FRIENDLY PARAMETERS SHOULD DICTATE THE DEVELOPMENT IN DEVELOPING COUNTRIES

PROF. DR. D. SWAMINADHAN

Global Chairman

World Intellectual Forum (WIF)

Hyderabad, India.

I0704172

Notion Press Media Pvt Ltd

No. 50, Chettiyar Agaram Main Road,
Vanagaram, Chennai, Tamil Nadu – 600 095

First Published by Notion Press 2021
Copyright © Prof. Dr. D. Swaminadhan 2021
All Rights Reserved.

ISBN 978-1-63940-333-2

The Historic Dandi March

Image Credit: https://www.pinterest.com/pin/17029304817074165/

The History of British Colonialism in India

Image Credit: YouTube.com

The Rise of the Muslim League

DEDICATION

The Author dedicates his Book to all those Common People who are struggling to become equals in enjoying their Constitutional Rights.

CONTENTS

CONTENTS

MESSAGES

 SAM PITRODA is an internationally respected development thinker, policymaker, inventor and entrepreneur who has spent over fifty-five years in telecom development.

Sam Pitroda Sun, May 9, 8:35 PM

to me, chaturvedi, d, Ian, Centre, Robert, Sharon, Thomas, cnrrao@jncasr.ac.in, Eduard, Swami-MSSRF, Marko, Sari, gila, michael@sustainabilitylabs.org, Homi, gulab@patrika.com, Dr, bircanuniver@lightmillenium.org, Nicholas, abdessatarbenmoussa@yahoo.fr, Shlomo, Birendra

Dear Dr.Swaminadhan,

Congratulations.

Your book on democracy looks interesting and would be of great value to young in India.I would like to learn more.

I am happy to inform you all that while in self quarantine at home in Chicago for the last 12 months, I wrote a book on "Redesign the World – A Global Call to Action". It is published by Penguin and available on Amazon. It is also available in the US,UK and other places. I am attaching a brief for your review.

Warm Regards.
Sam Pitroda

PREFACE

India won its Freedom in August 1947 from the British Colonial Rule primarily through a Non-violence method spear headed by Mahatma Gandhi, the Father of the Nation. After becoming Independent, India became a Sovereign, Socialist, Secular and Federal Democratic Country. It is the largest Democracy in the World. The Indian Constitution, which stands for national goals like Socialism and National Integration, was framed by the representatives of the Indian people over a long period of debates and discussions. It is the most detailed Constitution in the world.

They are modelled after the Westminster system for governing the State. The Union government is mainly composed of the executive, the legislature, and the judiciary. All powers are vested by the constitution in the prime minister, parliament and the supreme court. India is a Democracy with its Constitution guaranteeing to secure to all its citizens: Justice in social, economic and political spheres; Liberty of thought, expression, belief, faith and worship; Equality of status and opportunity; and to promote among them all Fraternity, assuring the dignity of individual and the unity and integrity of the nation. In the looks of the Indian Constitution, every citizen is equal. Democracy is defined as the government of the people, by the people and for the people. Democracy is considered the most acceptable form of government in which every individual participates consciously and in which the people remain the sovereign power determining their destiny. So, in a democracy, the people are the ultimate source of energy. That being the case, the Common man's status under the Indian Democracy and its Constitution becomes essential. The Common man includes Scheduled Castes, Scheduled Tribes, Minorities and Other Weaker Sections.

FOREWORD

In sitting down to write this Preface for Dr. Swaminadhan's important work on the inspiring story of Indian democracy, it has proven difficult not to fall into the cliché-padded trap of opening with the oft-quoted observation by Winston Churchill. Namely, that "Democracy is the worst form of government except for all the others." Indeed, while various emergency situations may require special provisions for a temporary concentration of power, in the long run, faith in the innate wisdom and native intelligence of "all the people" is the safer, more promising strategy.

In the context of western civilization, it is usually the ancient Greeks who are credited with launching us on the long and often tortuous adventure of experimenting with the idea of inclusion in governance. This idea, of expanding participation, even limited as it was at the time, represented a remarkable watershed. It came as a significant innovation in the annals of a long history of slowly producing new concepts, frameworks, modalities, and practices for organizing and managing human affairs. To appreciate the magnitude of the Greek innovation, recall that it emerged against a deeply entrenched context of the unquestionable view of absolute rulers as personifications of deities, or at the very least the only legitimate representatives of the Gods, on earth.

As it turns out, the wise intuition of Greek philosophers, and deep thinkers representing other wisdom traditions through the ages, is borne by the modern system sciences. Cybernetics, for example, focuses its theories on questions of how systems regulate themselves, how they adapt and evolve, how they self-organize and, more specifically, what are the structures and mechanisms that mediate their operations and conduct. Cybernetic theory established a fundamental, universal law of control. This law, known as "The Law of Requisite Variety," holds true for regulation in mechanical, physiological, biological, and societal systems alike. The law states that to be effective, a "controller" must embody the full variety of the system it attempts to control. Contemplate this powerful dictum and you will realize why dictatorships and other forms of autocratic regimes cannot be successful in the long run. They simply lack the requisite variety to accommodate the complex reality they propose to control!

More generally, we now understand that complex, self-organizing systems brains, societies, and ecosystems, including rainforests, coral reefs, and industrial economies alike—depend on their very complexity, their internal variety, for long-term vitality, viability, and vibrancy. Lasting stability in all such systems is, in fact, a direct function of complexity, of an inherent redundancy, which allows for the emergence and reemergence of different, and novel, configurations in response to changing circumstances and events. All the foregoing reinforces the still-too-fragile idea that open, transparent processes; responsive, agile structures; plurality of expression; and the equality of all individuals ought to constitute the cornerstones of social life. This is why allowing democracy to flourish is so important. Why it is critical to the future wellbeing of humanity and all other, all equally "living," components of the biosphere.

We are living during a challenging time. The adverse impacts of unthoughtful human activities now threaten all key components of our planet's ecosystems, including the wellbeing of our own species. The whole biospheric system is out of balance, as reflected in increasingly severe symptoms of profound malaise. These symptoms, which all too often are regarded as independent problems, are all interconnected and interdependent. The list includes: ozone depletion, climate change, loss of biodiversity, soil erosion and desertification, severe compromise of water resources, shrinkage of forest cover, growing income disparities within and between countries, and more. Change is clearly of the essence. But the required transformation is entirely unprecedented in scope. There simply is no previous experience with managing nine or ten billion people on the planet in a harmonious, peaceful, and enduringly abundant way. Most of our current institutions, mechanisms, and ways of comprehending and doing things, including existing national and international systems of governance, are not equal to the task.

At The Sustainability Laboratory, we work to advance the sustainability agenda through our research activities, educational programs, and project development initiatives. In the process, we have learnt two essential things. First, that addressing the sustainability challenge effectively requires the coherent integration of interrelated factors associated with five key domains. The Material Domain, which constitutes the basis for regulating the flow of materials and energy that underly existence; the Economic Domain, which provides the guiding framework for defining, creating and managing wealth; the Domain of Life, which provides the basis for appropriate behavior in the biosphere with respect to other forms of life; the Social Domain, which provides the basis for social interactions; and, last but not least, the Spiritual, or

Value Domain, which identifies the necessary attitudinal orientation and provides the basis for a universal code of ethics. A piecemeal approach—emphasizing some aspects while neglecting others—is unlikely to yield effective, lasting results.

Second, we have come to realize that peace, democracy and sustainability represent systemic states. As a system's state, each is the manifest result of a complex of interacting factors. Moreover, peace, democracy and sustainability are inexorably interrelated. You will not have peace without democracy, nor lasting sustainability without democracy and peace.

In the context of the social domain, and focusing on effective planetary governance, key policy and operational components of a comprehensive blueprint for change—some already reflected in ideas discussed in this book—must include the following imperatives:

- Foster tolerance as a cornerstone of social interactions

- Enshrine universal rights within a framework of planetary citizenship

- Provide for inclusion and effective democracy in governance

- Ensure equitable, shared, and responsible access to our planet's regenerative resources

- Establish cooperation as a basis for managing global issues and planetary commons

- Eliminate war and outlaw trade in weapons technologies

- Promote literacy, with emphasis on sustainability literacy, through education at all levels

- Embody sustainability-enhancing concepts in an effective planetary framework of legislation

This alone is a tall order, which swells in scope and proportion when you add all the factors that relate to the other four domains, and when you realize that all these must be acted on simultaneously. In addition, consider the fact that the kind of peaceful, sustainability-by-design revolution that is called for, can only be achieved by a concerted, collective, planet-wide effort. We are clearly faced with a daunting task. Especially in the face of prevailing fragmentation, dividing biases, cruel competition, and wide differences in levels of consciousness, literacy, capacity, and power that characterize the many, self-reinforcing, different identities of the world's often antagonistic, human groups.

This is where India's experience is of such vital importance. Today, India is the largest democracy in the world. The story of its heroic struggle for self-determination, freedom, and civil rights, and its astonishingly rapid emergence from a colonial subject to a global technology powerhouse, presents an uplifting story to the world. But Indian democracy, with its swelling population, still faces multiple challenges, and many of these are pointed out in this book. Such challenges range from caste discrimination, gender inequality, poverty, and illiteracy, to the task of the continuous integration of its multicultural, multilingual, multireligious, multiracial society. All of these represent, in a way, a microcosm of the planet as a whole.

Precisely because it faces so many vexing issues, India can lead as a giant laboratory. As it increasingly commits to a process of sustainable development, India can offer a showcase model to the world. The story of India's democracy can galvanize the world's people to join in establishing the concept of sustainability as the organizing principle on the planet. With its dignity, grace, beauty, creativity, and wisdom, India can lead humanity in a process of fulfilling its destiny.

An important point to bear in mind, in closing, is that democracy itself embodies a dynamic process. It is not a fixed, static condition, something to reach once and for all, then stop improving. Rather, it represents a history-long trajectory, of multiple, varied steps, some major and dramatic and some small but persistent, in an evolving saga—the story of humanity's tireless work on reforming, enhancing, strengthening, and enriching concepts and practices of good government. Democracy is nowhere near "perfect" yet, and observing governments around the world, even the best of them, suggests that we still have a long way to go. But the epic story goes on, and Dr. Swaminadhan's book provides some essential guiding posts. It joins other milestone contributions in the noble quest for a better world.

Michael Ben-Eli
The Sustainability Laboratory
New York
May 2021

ACKNOWLEDGEMENT

The Author expresses thanks to Dr. Michael Ben-Eli, The Sustainability Laboratory, New York for providing an excellent Foreword. The Author highly appreciate the stated goal of The Wikimedia Foundation of developing and maintaining open content, wiki-based projects and providing the entire contents of those projects to the public free of charge. In this context, I have freely used some images and write-ups from Wikipedia, the free encyclopaedia and the **Vikaspedia portal, IndiaDevelopmentGateway(InDG), initiative Centre for Development of Advanced Computing (C-DAC)** with the belief that they will not attract correct copy problems. I would also like to thank all those extended assistance in writing this book, especially my wife, Mrs D. Krishna Kumari, who needs special mention for her patience and encouragement throughout writing this Book.

– The Author

CHAPTER-I
INDIA–PAST AND PRESENT

India has a glorious past. It is a multicultural, multilingual, multireligious and multi communal country. But Unity in Diversity is its strength. India, since ancient times, has intermingled with many races and tribes. The pre-Aryans, the Indo-Aryans, the Hunas, the Turks, the Greeks, the Scythians, and others made India their home. Each ethnic group contributed to Indian social, cultural, artistic, literary, linguistic, and architectural richness.

People from all over the world came and settled in India. The Persians, followed by the Iranians, immigrated to India. Alexander, the great too, came to India in the hope of conquering it but went back after a battle with the Indian prince Porus. Genghis khan launched several invasions into the Indian subcontinent during Iltutmish's rule. Hiuen Tsang from China came to India to learn Buddhism and collect the wisdom of the religious texts.

In the 15th and 16th centuries, Europeans wanted to come to India to establish direct trade relations. The French, the Dutch, and the British came to India to trade their country's goods with Indian spices and other products. The British East India Company and subsequently the British Crown ruled over this country for almost 200 years.

After the battle of Plessey in 1757 and the Battle of Buxar in 1764, the British gradually transformed to become a significant political power.

After becoming Independent, India became a Sovereign, Socialist, Secular and Federal Democratic Country. It is the largest Democracy in the World. India is one of the oldest civilizations in the world, with a rich cultural heritage. It has achieved all-round socio-economic progress since its Independence in August 1947. It is the 7th largest country in the world. Bounded by the Great Himalayas in the north, it stretches southwards and tapers off into the Indian Ocean between the Bay of Bengal on the east and the Arabian Sea on the west. India is the most populous democracy in the world. And continues to have a vibrant media, an active civil society, a respected judiciary, and no significant human rights problems. India is a parliamentary secular democratic republic in which the President of India is the head of state and the Prime Minister of India is the head of government. It is based on the federal structure of government although the word is not used in the constitution itself.

More details about India are given in Annexure-I.

CHAPTER-II
INDIAN FREEDOM MOVEMENT

The Indian Freedom Movement was unique whose ultimate aim was to end the British Raj (1857–1947), and the East India Company rule (1757–1857) in India. The movement spanned a total of 90 years (1857–1947) considering movement against the British Indian Empire. The Indian Independence movement includes both protest (peaceful and non-violent) and militant (violent) mechanisms to root out the British Administration from India. The first organised militant movements were in Bengal, but they later took root in the newly formed Indian National Congress. The early part of the 20th century saw a more radical approach towards political self-rule. The last stages of the self-rule struggle from the 1920s onwards saw Congress adopt Mohandas Karamchand Gandhi's policy of nonviolence and civil disobedience, and several other campaigns. Nationalists like Subhash Chandra Bose, Bhagat Singh, Bagha Jatin, preached armed revolution to achieve self-rule. Poets and writers such as Subramania Bharati, RabindranathTagore, MuhaJosh Malihabadi, Mohammad Ali Jouhar, Bankim Chandra Chattopadhyay and Kazi Nazrul Islam used literature, poetry and speech as a tool for political awareness. Feminists such as Sarojini Naidu and Begum Rokeya promoted the emancipation of Indian women and their participation in national politics.

Dr. B. R. Ambedkar championed the cause of the disadvantaged sections of Indian society within the larger self-rule movement. The period of the Second World War saw the peak of the campaigns by the Quit India Movement led by Congress, and the Indian National Army movement led by Subhas Chandra Bose. The Indian self-rule movement was a mass-based movement that encompassed various sections of society. It also underwent a process of constant ideological evolution. Although the basic ideology of the movement was anti-colonial, it was supported by a vision of independent capitalist economic development coupled with a secular, democratic,, freedom of press republican, and civil-libertarian. Civil liberties normally include the freedom of conscience, freedom of religion, freedom of expression, freedom of assembly, the right to security and liberty, freedom of speech, the right to privacy, the right to equal treatment under the law and due process, the right to a fair trial, and the right to life. Other civil liberties include the right to own property, the right to defend oneself. After the 1930s, the movement took on a strong socialist orientation, owing to the influence of Bhagat Singh's demand of Purna Swaraj (Complete Self-Rule).The work of these various movements led ultimately to the Indian Independence Act 1947, which ended the in the creation of Pakistan. India remained a Dominion of the Crown until January 26 1950, when the Constitution of India came into force, establishing the Republic of India.

Imperial entities of India	
Dutch India	1605–1825
Danish India	1620–1869
French India	1668–1954
Portuguese India	
(1505–1961)	
Casa da India	1434–1833
Portuguese East India Company	1628–1633
British India	
(1612–1947)	
East India Company	1612–1757
Company rule in India	1757–1858
British Raj	1858–1947
British rule in Burma	1824–1948
Princely states	1721–1949
Partition of India	1947

CHAPTER-III
INDIAN DEMOCRACY

India is the largest democratic country in the world. Democracy is defined as a government of the people, by the people and for the people. Democracy is considered the finest form of government in which every individual participates consciously and in which the people remain the sovereign power determining their destiny. So, in a democracy, the people are the ultimate source of power and its success and failure depend on their wisdom, consciousness and vigilance. It is not possible for all the people in a big country like India to participate in the government. This is why they are required to exercise their franchise and elect their representatives at regular intervals. These representatives from the parliament legislate and form responsible government. Such governments can be either unitary or federal. In India the federal form having both a government at the centre responsible to the parliament and governments in the states elected and equally responsible to their legislative assemblies. But the people who participate in the election of their representatives must be educated enough to see what is good for them and who will be the right people to represent them. India became free only in 1947 after many years of colonial rule. In the following years India had her Constitution that declared India as a democratic federal republic. The first democratic election on the basis of universal adult franchise was held in 1952. However, during that election the people of India did not really have the necessary consciousness to understand Democracy. They did not have the education to choose between good and bad. Many people were victims of age-old poverty, ignorance and superstitions. Many of them did not even understand the difference between the British and the new rulers. However, the entire election process was held through a democratic process. Even today, after so many years, the people in India are not very much different, for many of them are illiterates. A large number of people are still below poverty level

Every form of government, whether democratic or dictatorship, has both advantages and disadvantages. Indian Democracy, without doubt, is very effective and proved to be very successful. It has successfully ensured individual freedom. But it has failed to completely eradicate poverty, injustices, social-evils and inequalities of the Indian society.

However, we must keep in mind that there is no better form of government than a Democratic government. It is, beyond doubt, a better form of government than that of aristocracy, dictatorship, and monarch. There is no better alternative to Democracy.

CHAPTER-IV
THE INDIAN CONSTITUTION

The Indian Constitution, which stands for national goals like Socialiarism and National Integration, was framed by the representatives of the Indian people over a long period of debates and discussions. It is the most detailed Constitution in the world. No other constitution has gone into such minute details as the Indian Constitution. The Constitution of India was framed by the Constituent Assembly, which was established in 1946. Dr. Rajendra Prasad was elected President of the Constituent Assembly. A Drafting Committee was appointed to draft the Constitution. Dr. B.R. Ambedkar was appointed the Chairman of the Drafting Committee. The Assembly met for 166 days and the Constitution was adopted on November 26, 1949. It came into force on January 26, 1950. It had incorporated some of the salient features of the British, Irish, Swiss, French, Canadian and the American Constitutions. The Constitution of India begins with a Preamble, which contains the basic ideals and principles of the Constitution. It lays down the objectives of the Constitution. The Constitution contains 395-Articles and 12 Schedules. A number of amendments passed have also become a part of this Constitution. The Constitution declares India to be a Sovereign, Secular, Socialist, and a Democratic Republic. At the same time, India has federal features.

The powers of the government are divided between the central government and the State governments. The Constitution demarcates the powers of the central and state governments into different lists of subjects. These lists are called the Union List, the State List and the Concurrent List. The Constitution provides for an independent and impartial judiciary and the Supreme Court is the highest court of the country. It decides disputes between the people and the government. The Constitution provides for the establishment of parliamentary form of government in India.

The President is the nominal head of the state. In actual practice the administration is run by the Prime Minister and the Council of Ministers. The council of Ministers is responsible to the Parliament. The Constitution of India guarantees Fundamental Rights to all its citizens. They have Right to Equality, Right to Freedom, right against Exploitation, Right to Freedom of Religion, Cultural and Educational Rights and Right to Constitutional Remedies.Taking inspiration from the Constitution" of Ireland, framer of our Constitution included the directive principles directions given to the central government and state governments to adopt such policies which would help establish a just society in our country. There are times when the country could not be run as in ordinary times. To cope with such difficult times, the Constitution provides for the emergency provisions, which are it's another important feature. Yet another unique feature of our Constitution is that it is not as rigid as the American Constitution or as flexible as the British Constitution. It means it is partly rigid and partly flexible. And so it can easily change and grow with the change of times. Thus, Indian Constitution in keeping with its size has a number of distinctive features.

It is heartening to note that various constitutional safe guards are in the Constitution for the welfare and development of the weaker sections like Scheduled Castes and Scheduled Tribes which include mostly the Common people.

Further Details are provided in Annexure-II

CHAPTER- V
THE INDIAN PARLIAMENT

The Parliament of India is the supreme legislative body of the Republic of India. It is a legislature composed of the President of India and the two houses: the Rajya Sabha (Council of States) and the Lok Sabha (House of the People). The President in his role as head of legislature has full powers to summon and prorogue either house of Parliament or to dissolve Lok Sabha. The president can exercise these powers only upon the advice of the Prime Minister and his Union Council of Ministers.Those elected or nominated (by the President) to either house of Parliament are referred to as Members of Parliament (MP). The Members of Parliament, Lok Sabha are directly elected by the Indian public voting in Single-member districts and the Members of Parliament, Rajya Sabha are elected by the members of all State Legislative Assembly by proportional representation. The Parliament has a sanctioned strength of 543 in Lok Sabha and 245 in Rajya Sabha including the 12 nominees from the expertise of different fields of science, culture, art and history. The Parliament meets at Sansad Bhavan in New Delhi.Modelled after the Westminster system for governing the state the Union government is mainly composed of the executive, the legislature, and the judiciary, in which all powers are vested by the constitution in the prime minister, parliament and the supreme court. The president of India is the head of state and the commander-in-chief of the Indian Armed Forces whilst the elected prime minister acts as the head of the executive, and is responsible for running the Union government. The parliament is bicameral in nature, with the Lok Sabha being the lower house, and the Rajya Sabha the upper house. The judiciary systematically contains an apex supreme court, 24 high courts, and several district courts, all inferior to the Supreme Court. The basic civil and criminal laws governing the citizens of India are set down in major parliamentary legislation, such as the civil procedure code, the penal code, and the criminal procedure code. Similar to the Union government, individual State governments each consist of executive, legislative and judiciary. The legal system as applicable to the Union and individual State governments is based on the English Common and Statutory Law. The full name of the country is the *Republic of India*. India and Bharat are equally official short names for the Republic of India in the Constitution, and both names appears on legal banknotes, in treaties and in legal cases. The terms "Union Government", "Central Government" and "*Bhārat Sarkār*" are often used officially and unofficially to refer to the Government of India. The term *New Delhi* is commonly used as a metonym for the Union government as the seat of the government is in New Delhi.

CHAPTER-VI

THE INDIAN JUDICIARY SYSTEM

India has **a single integrated judicial system.** The judiciary in India has a **pyramid**al **structure with the Supreme Court (SC)** at **the top.** High Courts are below the SC, and below them are the district and subordinate courts. The lower courts function under the direct superintendence of the higher courts. The Indian Judiciary administers a *common law system* in which customs, securities and legislation, all codify the law of the land. It has, in fact, inherited the legacy of the legal system established by the then colonial powers and the princely states since the mid-19th century, and has partly retained the characteristics of practices from the ancient and medieval times.The Indian Judicial system is totally managed and administrated by officers of judicial service unlike in the past when civil service officers also were part of judicial system. The expression judicial service means a service consisting exclusively of persons intended to fill the post of district judge and other civil judicial posts inferior to the post of district judge. The Judges of Subordinate Judiciary is appointed by the governor on recommendation of the High Court. Judges of the High Court and Supreme Court are appointed by the President of India on the recommendation of a collegium. The Judicial system of India is classified into three levels with subsidiary parts. The Supreme Court of India, also known as the Apex Court, is the top court and the last appellate court in India, and the Chief Justice of India is its top authority. High Courts are the top judicial bodies in the states controlled and managed by Chief Justices of States. Below the High Court are District Courts, also known as subordinate courts, controlled and managed by the District & Sessions Judges. The subordinate court system is further classified into two: the civil court of which a Sub-Judge is the head followed by the munsif court at the lower level, and the criminal court headed by Chief Judicial/Metropolitan Magistrate at top and followed by ACJM/ACMM & JM/MM at the lower level. The other courts are the executive and revenue courts which are managed and controlled by state government through the district magistrates and commissioners, respectively. Although the executive courts are not the part of judiciary but various provisions and judgements empower the High Courts and the Session Judges to inspect or direct the working of executive courts.

The Ministry of Law & Justice at the Union level is responsible for raising issues before parliament for the proper functioning of the judiciary. The Ministry of Law & Justice has complete jurisdiction to deal with the issues of any courts of India, from SC to subordinate and Executive Courts. It also deals with the appointment of Judges of the High Courts and the Supreme Court. At the state level, the law departments of the states deal with the issues of the High Court and the Subordinate Courts. The constitution provides for the single unified judiciary in India.

The relation between Judiciary and Constitution is that Constitution empowers Judiciary to act as the Guardian of the Law. Therefore in common language can say Judiciary is itself a constitution but this does not mean that the court have unlimited power because in India the doctrine of Constitutionalism is also applied. However, there are number of provisions which specifically deals with the Indian Judiciary role, power & function and appointment of officers.

CHAPTER- VII

PROMINENT INDIAN LEADERS WITH THE PRO-COMMON MAN INTEREST

I. THE FATHER OF THE NATION

Mahatma Gandhi

Mohandas Karamchand Gandhi was the leader of the Indian Independence movement against British colonial rule. Employing nonviolent civil disobedience, Gandhi led India to independence and inspired movements for civil rights and freedom across the world. The honorific **Mahātmā** was applied to him first in 1914 in South Africa – is now used worldwide. In India, he was also called **Bapu**, a term that he preferred and is known as the Father of the Nation. Born and raised in a Hindu merchant caste family in coastal Gujarat, India, and trained in law at the Inner Temple, London, Gandhi first employed nonviolent civil disobedience as an expatriate lawyer in South Africa, in the resident Indian community's struggle for civil rights. After his return to India in 1915, he set about organising peasants, farmers, and urban labourers to protest against excessive land-tax and discrimination. Assuming leadership of the Indian National Congress in 1921, Gandhi led nationwide campaigns for various social causes and for achieving *Swaraj* or self-rule. Gandhi led Indians in challenging the British-imposed salt tax with the 400 km (250 mi) Dandi Salt March in 1930, and later in calling for the British to Quit India in 1942. He was imprisoned for many years, upon many occasions, in both South Africa and India. He lived modestly in a self-sufficient residential community and wore the traditional Indian *dhoti* and shawl, woven with yarn hand-spun on a *charkha*. He ate simple vegetarian food, and also undertook long fasts as a means of both self-purification and political protest. Gandhi's vision of an independent India based on religious pluralism was challenged in the early 1940s by a new Muslim nationalism which was demanding a separate Muslim homeland carved out of India. In August 1947, Britain granted independence, but the British Indian Empire was partitioned into two dominions, a Hindu-majority India and Muslim-majority Pakistan. As many displaced Hindus, Muslims, and Sikhs made their way to their new lands, religious violence broke out, especially in the Punjab and Bengal. Eschewing the official celebration of independence in Delhi, Gandhi visited the affected areas, attempting to provide solace. In the months following, he undertook several fasts unto death to stop religious violence. The last of these, undertaken on January 12 1948 when he was 78, also had the indirect goal of pressuring India to pay out some cash assets owed to Pakistan. Some Indians thought Gandhi was too accommodating. Among them was Nathuram Godse, a Hindu nationalist, who assassinated Gandhi on January 30 1948 by firing three bullets into his chest. Captured along with many of his co-

conspirators and collaborators, Godse and his co-conspirator, Narayan Apte were tried, convicted and executed while many of their other accomplices were given prison sentences. Gandhi's birthday, October 2, is commemorated in India as Gandhi Jayanti, a national holiday, and worldwide as the International Day of Non violence.

II. THE ARCHITECT OF MODERN INDIA

JAWAHARLAL NEHRU

Pt.Jawaharlal Nehru was born in Allabahad on November 14, 1889. He received his early education at home under private tutors. At the age of fifteen, he went to England and after two years at Harrow, joined Cambridge University, where he took his trips in Natural Sciences. He was later called to the Bar from Inner Temple. He returned to India in 1912 and plunged straight into politics. Even as a student, he had been interested in the struggle of all nations who suffered under foreign domination. He took keen interest in the Sinn Fein Movement in Ireland. In India, he was inevitably drawn into the struggle for independence. In 1912, he attended the Bankipore Congress as a delegate, and became Secretary of the Home Rule League, Allahabad in 1919. In 1916 he had his first meeting with Mahatma Gandhi and felt immensely inspired by him. He organised the first Kisan March in Pratapgarh District of Uttar Pradesh in 1920. He was twice imprisoned in connection with the Non-Cooperation Movement of 1920-22. Pt. Nehru became the General

Secretary of the All India Congress Committee in September 1923. He toured Italy, Switzerland, England, Belgium, Germany and Russia in 1926. In Belgium, he attended the Congress of Oppressed Nationalities in Brussels as an official delegate of the Indian National Congress. He also attended the tenth anniversary celebrations of the October Socialist Revolution in Moscow in 1927. Earlier, in 1926, at the Madras Congress, Nehru had been instrumental in committing the Congress to the goal of Independence. While leading a procession against the Simon commission, he was lathi-charged in Lucknow in 1928. On August 29, 1928 he attended the All-Party Congress and was one of the signatories to the Nehru Report on Indian Constitutional Reform, named after his father Shri Motilal Nehru. The same year, he also founded the 'Independence for India League', which advocated complete severance of the British connection with India, and became its General Secretary. In 1929, Pt. Nehru was elected President of the Lahore Session of the Indian National Congress, where complete independence for the country was adopted as the goal. He was imprisoned several times during 1930-35 in connection with the Salt Satyagraha and other movements launched by the Congress. He completed his 'Autobiography' in Almora Jail on February 14, 1935. After release, he flew to Switzerland to see his ailing wife and visited London in February-March, 1936. He also visited Spain in July 1938, when the country was in the throes of the Civil War. Just before the court-break of the Second World War, he visited China too. On October 31, 1940 Pt. Nehru was arrested for offering individual Satyagraha to protest against India's forced participation in war. He was released along with the other leaders in December 1941. On August 7, 1942 Pt. Nehru moved the historic 'Quit India' resolution at the AICC. Session in Bombay. On August 8, 1942 he was arrested along with other leaders and taken to Ahmednagar Fort. This was his longest and also his last detention. In all, he suffered imprisonment nine times. After his release in January 1945, he organized legal defence for those officers and men of the INA charged with treason. In March 1946, Pt. Nehru toured South East Asia. He was elected President of the Congress for the fourth time on July 6, 1946 and again for three more terms from 1951 to 1954.

III. THE ARCHITECT OF THE INDIAN CONSTITUTION

DR B R AMBEDKAR

Babasaheb Dr Bhimrao Ramji Ambedkar was a scholar, a social reformer and a leader who dedicated his life to eradicating social inequality in India. He established an India of equals, a country which provided greater opportunities for people who were historically disadvantaged. It takes courage to break free from the shackles of social inequality. It takes enormous amounts of courage to believe that things can change. It takes a leader to fight these inequalities and establish a new social order.

The Babasaheb's family was from the Mahar community and came from the Ambavade town of Mandan gad Taluka in the Ratnagiri district of Maharashtra. However, he was born in the military cantonment town of Mhow, now in Madhya Pradesh on April 14 1891 as his father was then a Subedar Major with the Mahar Regiment of the Indian Army. He went to a government school where children from lower castes, regarded as untouchables, were segregated and given little attention or assistance by the teachers and not allowed to sit inside the classroom. Students from the community had to go without water if the peon did not report for duty. In 1894, Babasaheb's family moved to Satara in Maharashtra, and his mother passed away shortly after their family moved to Satara. His teacher Mahadev Ambedkar, a Brahmin, was fond of him and changed his surname from 'Ambavadekar' to his own surname 'Ambedkar' in school records. In 1897, Babasaheb's family moved to Bombay. He married Ramabai in 1906 when he was 15 and Ramabai nine years old. This, however, did not deter him in his academic pursuits as he passed the matriculation examination in 1907 and entered the Elphinstone College the following year, becoming the first person from an untouchable community to do so. By 1912, he obtained his degree in Economics and Political Science from Bombay University and took up employment with the government of the princely state of Baroda. This opened up new avenues for Babasaheb as he got an opportunity to pursue his post-graduation at the Columbia University in the United States in 1913 through a Baroda State Scholarship instituted by the Gaekwads of Baroda awarding £11.50 (Sterling) per month for three years.

He passed his MA exam in June 1915 majoring in Economics, with Sociology, History, Philosophy and Anthropology as other subjects of study; he presented a thesis 'Ancient Indian Commerce'. In 1916 he offered another MA thesis, 'National Dividend of India - A Historic and Analytical Study'. On May 9, he read his paper 'Castes in India: Their Mechanism, Genesis and Development' before a seminar conducted by the anthropologist Alexander Goldenweiser. In October 1916 he studied for the Bar examination at Gray's Inn, and enrolled at the London School of Economics where he started work on a doctoral thesis. In June 1917 he was obliged to go back to India as the term of his scholarship from Baroda ended.

However, he was given permission to return and submit his thesis within four years. He was appointed as Military Secretary to the Gaekwads of Baroda but had to quit within a short time, pushing him into financial hardship.

In 1918 he became Professor of Political Economy in the Sydenham College of Commerce and Economics in Bombay and though he was very popular with his students, he had to face discrimination from his colleagues. It was during this period that Babasaheb started taking greater interest in politics as he was invited to testify before the South borough Committee, which was preparing the Government of India Act 1919. During this hearing, he argued for creating separate electorates and reservations for untouchables and other religious communities.

In 1920, he began publication of the weekly Mooknayak in Mumbai with the help of Chhatrapati Shahu Maharaj, Maharaja of Kolhapur. A social reformer, the Maharaja played a pioneering role in opening up education and employment to people of all castes. Babasaheb continued to fight for justice for the untouchables in the years that followed, as a practicing lawyer and as a social reformer.

By 1927, he decided to launch active movements against untouchability and espousing access to public drinking water resources and the right to enter Hindu temples. He led a Satyagraha in Mahad to fight for the right of the untouchable community to draw water from the main water tank of the town.

He was appointed to the Bombay Presidency Committee to work with the Simon Commission in 1925. While the Commission had faced protests across India and its report was largely ignored, Babasaheb himself wrote a separate set of constitutional recommendations for the future. Babasaheb was invited to attend the Second Round Table Conference in London in 1932 but Mahatma Gandhi was opposed to a separate electorate for untouchables as this would split the nation.

In 1932, the British announced a Communal Award of a separate electorate, Gandhi ji protested by fasting while imprisoned in the Yerwada Central Jail of Poona. This resulted in an agreement widely known as the Poona Pact in which Gandhi ji ended his fast and Babasaheb dropped his demand for a separate electorate. Instead, a certain number of seats were reserved specifically for the 'Depressed Class'. In 1935, Babasaheb was appointed principal of the Government Law College in Mumbai and continued in that position for two years. He lost his wife Ramabai during this period and this marked the beginning of an important chapter in Babasaheb's life. On October 13 that year, he announced his intention to convert to a different religion and exhorted his followers to leave Hinduism while speaking at the Yeola Conversion Conference in Nasik and repeated his message all through the country. In 1936, Babasaheb Ambedkar founded the Independent Labour Party, which contested the 1937 Bombay election to the Central Legislative Assembly for the 13 reserved and 4 general seats, securing 11 and 3 seats respectively. He served on the Defence Advisory Committee and the Viceroy's Executive Council as Minister for Labour during this period. This is also the period when Babasaheb wrote extensively on the condition of Dalits and the caste system in Hindu society. During this period, Babasaheb renamed his party as the Scheduled Castes Federation, which later evolved into the Republican Party of India.

He was initially elected to the Constituent Assembly from Bengal but his seat went to Pakistan following the Partition of India. He was subsequently elected from the Bombay Presidency in place of a senior jurist Jaykar, ahead of Shri GV Mavalankar.

India became an Independent nation on August 15, 1947 and Babasaheb Ambedkar was appointed as the Union Law Minister and Chairman of the Constitution Drafting Committee, which was given the responsibility to write India's new Constitution.

Babasaheb Ambedkar's text provided constitutional guarantees and protections for a wide range of civil liberties for individual citizens, including freedom of religion, the abolition of untouchability and the outlawing of all forms of discrimination. Granville Austin described the Indian Constitution as 'first and foremost a social document'. He argued for equality and also won wide support for introducing a system of reservations of jobs for members of scheduled castes and scheduled tribes in the civil services, schools and colleges. This was aimed at providing a voice to people who had suffered grave injustices through centuries. The Constituent Assembly formally approved the draft Constitution on November 26 1949 and Babasaheb's greatest work, the Indian Constitution, became our way of life on January 26 1950.

The struggle was a part of Babasaheb's life as he had to work hard for everything he achieved. While he is remembered for his relentless crusade for a new social order, the Indian nation shall always remain indebted to him for giving us a Constitution that defines our core values as a nation. He was the man who made us a nation of equals.

IV. IRON MAN OF INDIA

(From Wikipedia, the free encyclopaedia)

Vallabhbhai Jhaverbhai Patel

Popularly known as **Sardar Patel**, served as the first Deputy Prime Minister of India. He was an Indian barrister, and a senior leader of the Indian National Congress who played a leading role in the country's struggle for independence and guided its integration into a united, independent nation. In India and elsewhere, he was often called *Sardar*, meaning "chief" in Hindi, Urdu, and Persian. He acted as Home Minister during the political integration of India and the Indo-Pakistani War of1947.

Patel was born in Nadiad District Kheda and raised in the countryside of the state of Gujarat. He was a successful lawyer. He subsequently organised peasants from Kheda, Borsad,and Bardoli in Gujarat in non-violent civil disobedience against the British Raj, becoming one of the most influential leaders in Gujarat. He was appointed as the 49th President of Indian National Congress, organising the party for elections in 1934 and 1937 while promoting the Quit India Movement.

As the first Home Minister and Deputy Prime Minister of India, Patel organised relief efforts for refugees fleeing to Punjab and Delhi from Pakistan and worked to restore peace. He led the task of forging a united India, successfully integrating into the newly independent nation those British colonial provinces that had been "allocated" to India. Besides those provinces that had been under direct British rule, approximately

565 self-governing princely states had been released from British suzerainty by the Indian Independence Act of 1947. Patel persuaded almost every princely state to accede to India. His commitment to national integration in the newly independent country was total and uncompromising, earning him the Name"Iron Man of India". He is also remembered as the "patron saint of India's civil servants" for having established the modern all-India services system. He is also called the "Unifier of India". The Statue of Unity, the world's tallest statue, was dedicated to him on 31 October 2018 which is approximately 182 metres (597 ft) in height.

In 1909 Patel's wife Jhaverba was hospitalised in Bombay (present-day Mumbai) to undergo major surgery for cancer. Her health suddenly worsened and, despite successful emergency surgery, she died in the hospital. Patel was given a note informing him of his wife's demise as he was cross-examining a witness in court. According to witnesses, Patel read the note, pocketed it, and continued his cross-examination and won the case. He broke the news to others only after the proceedings had ended. Patel decided against marrying again. At the age of 36, he journeyed to England and enrolled at the Middle Temple Inn in London. Completing a 36-month course in 30 months, Patel finished at the top of his class despite having had no previous college background. Returning to India, Patel settled in Ahmedabad and became one of the city's most successful barristers, wearing European-style clothes.

Patel supported Gandhi's Non-cooperation movement and toured the state to recruit more than 300,000 members and rise over Rs. 1.5 million in funds. Helped to organise bonfires in Ahmedabad in which British goods were burned, Patel threw in all his English-style clothes. Along with his daughter Mani and son Dahya, he switched completely too wearing khadi, the locally produced cotton clothing. Patel also supported Gandhi's controversial suspension of resistance in the wake of the Chauri Chaura incident. In Gujarat, he worked extensively in the following years against alcoholism, untouchability, and caste discrimination, as well as for the empowerment of women. In the Congress, he was a resolute supporter of Gandhi against his Swarajist critics.

While Nehru, Rajagopalachari, and Maulana Azad initially criticised Gandhi's proposal for an all-out campaign of civil disobedience to force the British to quit India, Patel was its most fervent supporter. Arguing that the British would retreat from India as they had from Singapore and Burma, Patel urged that the campaign start without any delay. Though feeling that the British would not leave immediately, Patel favoured an all-out rebellion that would galvanise the Indian people, who had been divided in their response to the war, In Patel's view, such a rebellion would force the British to concede that continuation of colonial rule had no support in India, and thus speed the transfer of power to Indians. He raised funds and prepared a second tier of command as a precaution against the arrest of national leaders.

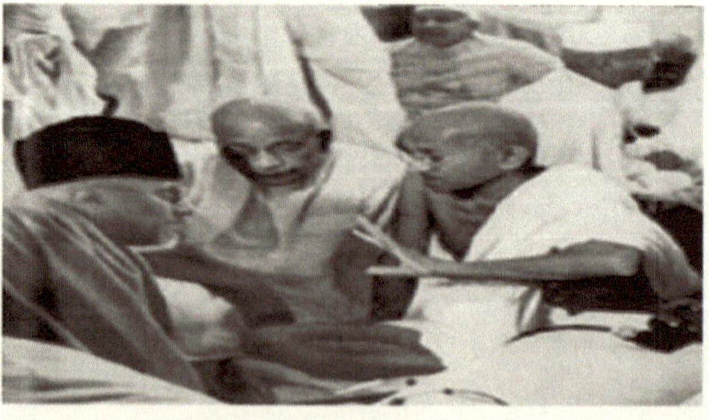

Maulana Azad, Jamnalal Bajaj, Patel (third from left, in the foreground), Subhash Chandra Bose and other Congressmen at Wardha.

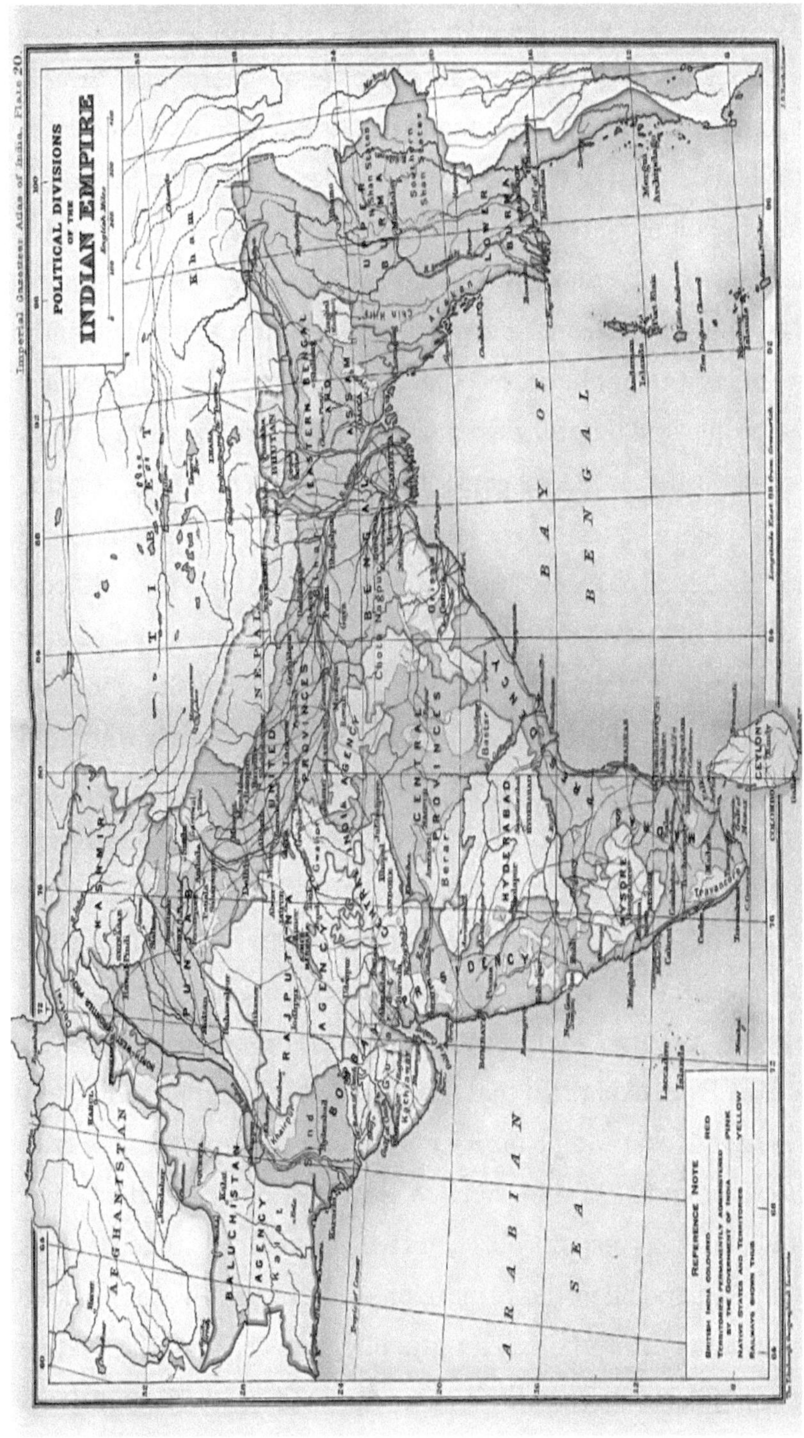

POLITICAL DIVISIONS
OF THE
INDIAN EMPIRE
AFGHANISTAN
BALUCHISTAN
KASHMIR
PUNJAB
RAJPUTANA AGENCY
UNITED PROVINCES
NEPAL
BHUTAN
EASTERN BENGAL AND ASSAM
BENGAL
CENTRAL INDIA AGENCY
CENTRAL PROVINCES
BOMBAY
HYDERABAD
MYSORE
MADRAS PRESIDENCY
BAY OF BENGAL
ARABIAN SEA
CEYLON
BURMA
REFERENCE NOTE

Patel took charge of the integration of the princely states into India. This achievement formed the cornerstone of Patel's popularity in the post-independence era. Even today he is remembered as the man who united India. He is, in this regard, compared to Otto von Bismarck who unified the many German states in 1871. Under the plan of 3 June, more than 565 princely states were given the option of joining either India or Pakistan, or choosing independence. Indian nationalists and large segments of the public feared that if these states did not accede, most of the people and territory would be fragmented. The Congress, as well as senior British officials, considered Patel the best man for the task of achieving conquest of the princely states by the Indian dominion. Gandhi had said to Patel, "[T]he problem of the States is so difficult that you alone can solve it". Patel was considered a statesman of integrity with the practical acumen and resolve to accomplish a monumental task. He asked V. P. Menon, a senior civil servant with whom he had worked on the partition of India, to become his right-hand man as chief secretary of the States Ministry. On 6 August 1947, Patel began lobbying the princes, attempting to make them receptive towards dialogue with the future government and forestall potential conflicts. Patel used social meetings and unofficial surroundings to engage most of the monarchs, inviting them to lunch and tea at his home in Delhi. At these meetings, Patel explained that there was no inherent conflict between the Congress and the princely order. Patel invoked the patriotism of India's monarchs, asking them to join in the independence of their nation and act as responsible rulers who cared about the future of their people. He persuaded the princes of 565 states of the impossibility of independence from the Indian republic, especially in the presence of growing opposition from their subjects. He proposed favourable terms for the merger, including the creation of *privy purses* for the rulers' descendants. While encouraging the rulers to act out of patriotism, Patel did not rule out force. Stressing that the princes would need to accede to India in good faith, he set a deadline of 15 August 1947 for them to sign the instrument of accession document. All but three of the states willingly merged into the Indian union; only Jammu and Kashmir, Junagadh, and Hyderabad did not fall into his plan.

British Indian Empire in 1909

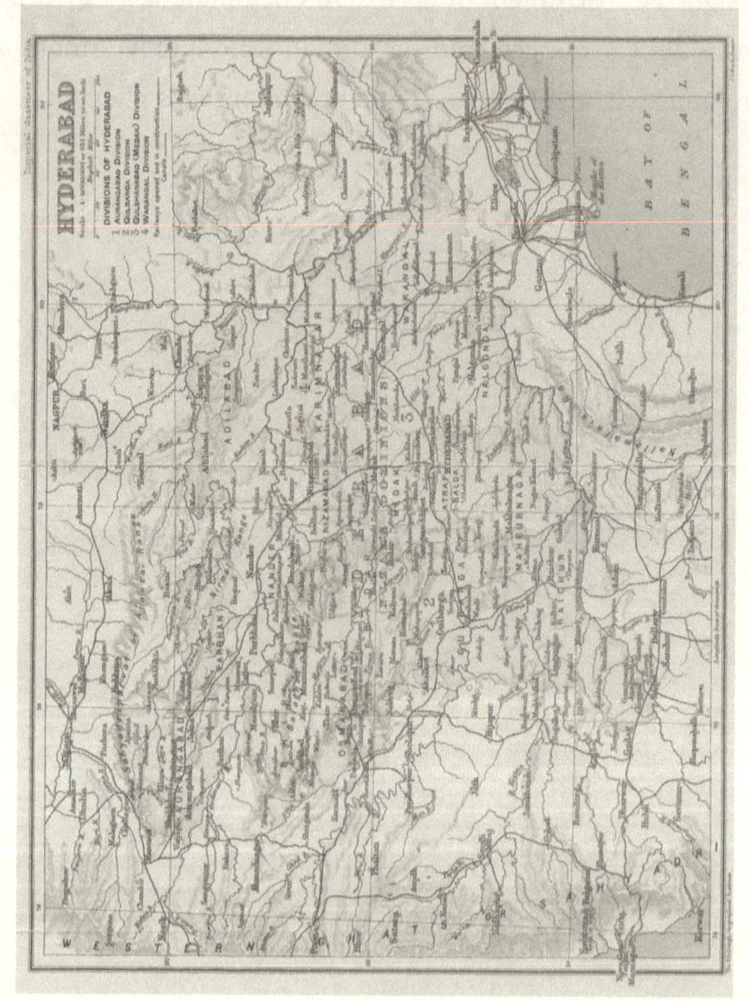

Hyderabad state in 1909. Its area stretched over large parts of the current Indian states of Telangana, Karnataka, and Maharashtra.

V. IRON LADY OF INDIA

Smt. Indira Gandhi

Born on November 19, 1917 in an illustrious family, Smt. Indira Gandhi was the daughter of Pt. Jawaharlal Nehru. She studied at prime institutions like Ecole Nouvelle, Bex (Switzerland), Ecole Internationale, Geneva, Pupils' Own School, Poona and Bombay, Badminton School, Bristol, Vishwa Bharati, Shantiniketan and Somerville College, Oxford. She was conferred Honorary doctoral degree by a host of Universities globally. With an impressive academic background she also got the Citation of Distinction from the Columbia University. Smt. Indira Gandhi was actively involved in the freedom struggle. In her childhood, she founded the 'Bal Charkha Sangh' and in 1930, the 'Vanar Sena' of children to help the Congress party during the Non-Cooperation Movement. She was imprisoned in September 1942, and worked in riot-affected areas of Delhi in 1947 under Gandhi's guidance. She got married to Feroze Gandhi on March 26, 1942 and had two sons. Smt. Gandhi became a Member, Congress Working Committee and Central Election of the party in 1955. In 1958 she was appointed as a Member for Central Parliamentary Board of Congress. She was the Chairperson, National Integration Council of A.I.C.C. and President, All India Youth Congress, 1956 and Women's Dept. A.I.C.C. She became the President, Indian National Congress in 1959 and served till 1960 and then again from January 1978. She had been Minister for Information and Broadcasting (1964- 1966). Then she held the highest office as the Prime Minister of India from January 1966 to March 1977. Concurrently, she was the Minister for

Atomic Energy from September 1967 to March 1977. She also held the additional charge of the Ministry of External Affairs from September 5, 1967 to February 14, 1969. Smt. Gandhi headed the Ministry of Home Affairs from June 1970 to November 1973 and Minister for Space from June 1972 to March 1977. From January 1980 she was Chairperson, Planning Commission. She again chaired the prime Minister's Office from January 14, 1980. Smt. Indira Gandhi was associated with a large number of organisations and institutions, like Kamala Nehru Memorial Hospital, Gandhi Smarak Nidhi and Kasturba Gandhi Memorial Trust. She was the Chairperson of Swaraj Bhavan Trust. She was also associated with Bal Sahyog, Bal Bhavan Board and Children's National Museum in 1955. Smt. Gandhi founded the Kamala Nehru Vidyalaya in Allahabad. She was also associated with certain big institutions like Jawaharlal Nehru University and North-Eastern University during 1966-77. She also served as a Member of Delhi University Court, Indian Delegation to UNESCO (1960-64), Member, Executive Board of UNESCO from 1960-64 and Member, National Defence Council, 1962. She was also associated with Sangeet Natak Academy, National Integration Council, Himalayan Mountaineering Institute, Dakshina Bharat Hindi Prachar Sabha, Nehru Memorial Museum and Library Society and Jawaharlal Nehru Memorial Fund.

Smt. Gandhi also became a Member of Rajya Sabha in August 1964 and served till February 1967. She was the Member of Lok Sabha during fourth, fifth and sixth sessions. She was elected to the Seventh Lok Sabha from Rae Bareli (U.P.) and Medak (Andhra Pradesh) in January 1980. She chose to retain the Medak seat and relinquished the Rae Bareli seat. She was chosen as the leader of the Congress Parliamentary Party in 1967-77 and again in January 1980.

Interested in a wide array of subjects, she viewed life as an integrated process, where activities and interests are different facets of the whole, not separated into compartments or labelled under different heads.

She had many achievements to her credit. She was the recipient of Bharat Ratna in 1972, Mexican Academy Award for Liberation of Bangladesh (1972), 2nd Annual Medal, FAO (1973) and Sahitya Vachaspati (Hindi) by Nagari Pracharini Sabha in 1976. Smt. Gandhi also received Mothers' Award, U.S.A. in 1953, Islbella d'Este Award of Italy for outstanding work in diplomacy and Yale University's Howland Memorial Prize. For two consecutive years in 1967 and 1968 she was the woman most admired by the French according to a poll by the French Institute of Public Opinion. According to a special Gallup Poll Survey in the U.S.A. in 1971 she was the most admired person in the world. Diploma of Honour was conferred to her by the Argentine Society in 1971 for the Protection of Animals.

Her famous publications include 'The Years of Challenge' (1966-69), 'The Years of Endeavour' (1969-72), 'India' (London) in 1975; 'Inde' (Lausanne) in 1979 and numerous other collections of speeches and writings. She travelled widely in India and all over the world. Smt. Gandhi also visited neighbours like Afghanistan, Bangladesh, Bhutan, Burma, China, Nepal and Sri Lanka. She paid official visits to countries like France, German Democratic Republic, Federal Republic of Germany, Guyana, Hungary, Iran, Iraq and Italy. Smt. Gandhi was one to visit majority of the countries like Algeria, Argentina, Australia, Austria Belgium, Brazil, Bulgaria, Canada, Chile, Czechoslovakia, Bolivia and Egypt. She paid visits to many European, American and Asian nationals like Indonesia, Japan, Jamaica, Kenya, Malaysia, Mauritius, Mexico, Netherlands, New Zealand, Nigeria, Oman, Poland, Romania,

Singapore, Switzerland, Syria, Sweden, Tanzania, Thailand, Trinidad and Tobago, U.A.E., the United Kingdom, U.S.A., U.S.S.R., Uruguay, Venezuela, Yugoslavia, Zambia and Zimbabwe. She also marked her presence in the United Nations Headquarters.

VI. FATHER OF GLOBALISATION IN INDIA

Shri PV Narasimha Rao
Former Prime Minister of India

After the assassination of Shri Rajiv Gandhi, the Congress Party came to power and Shri P.V.Narasimha Rao, senior Congress Leader emerged as the concusses candidate for Prime Minister Ship. Thus he took over as Prime Minister of India. His tenure was from June 21,1991 to May 16, 1996. Son of Shri P. Ranga Rao, Shri P.V. Narasimha Rao was born on June 28, 1921 at Karimnagar. He studied in Osmania University, Hyderabad, Bombay University and the Nagpur University. A widower, Shri P.V. Narasimha Rao is the father of three sons and five daughters. Being an agriculturist and an advocate, he joined politics and held some important portfolios. He was the Minister of Law and Information, 1962-64; Law and Endowments, 1964-67; Health and Medicine, 1967 and Education, 1968-71,Government of Andhra Pradesh. He was the Chief Minister, Andhra Pradesh, 1971-73; General Secretary, All India Congress Committee, 1975-76; Chairman, Telugu Academy, Andhra Pradesh, 1968-74; Vice-President, Dakshin Bharat Hindi Prachar Sabha, Madras,from 1972. He was also Member, Andhra Pradesh Legislative Assembly, 1957-77; Member, Lok Sabha. He was the

Minister for External Affairs from January 14, 1980 to July 18, 1984; Minister of Home Affairs from July 19, 1984 to December 31, 1984 and the Minister of Defence from December 31, 1984 to September 25, 1985. He then assumed charge as Minister of Human Resource Development on September 25, 1985.He was elected to Eighth Lok Sabha from Ramtek in December, 1984. As Chairman, Public Accounts Committee, 1978-79 he participated in a Conference on South Asia convened by the School of Asian and African Studies, London University. Shri Rao also Chaired Bhartiya Vidya Bhavan. A man of many interests, he likes music, cinema and theatre. His special interest lies in Indian philosophy and culture, writing fiction and political commentary, learning languages, writing poems in Telugu and Hindi and keeping abreast of literature in general. He has successfully published 'Sahasra Phani', a Hindi translation of late Shri Viswanatha Satyanarayana's famous Telegu Novel 'Veyi Padagalu' published by Jnanpith; 'Abala Jeevitam', Telugu translation of late Shri Hari Narayan Apte's famous Marathi Novel, "Pan Lakshat Kon ghetto", published by the Central Sahitya Academy. He translated other famous works from Marathi to Telugu and from Telugu to Hindi, and published many articles in different magazines mostly under a pen name. He lectured at Universities in the U.S.A. and West Germany on political matters and allied subjects. As Minister of External Affairs he travelled extensively to U.K., West Germany, Switzerland, Italy and Egypt in 1974. During the period when he was Minister of External Affairs, Shri Rao successfully brought to bear his scholarly background and rich political and administrative experience on the field of international diplomacy. He chaired the III Conference of UNIDO in New Delhi in January 1980, within a few days of assuming charge. He also chaired a meeting of the Group of 77 at New York in March 1980. More recently, his role of the

Conference of Foreign Ministers of Nonaligned Countries in February 1981 earned him wide appreciation. Shri Rao has shown keen personal interest in international economic issues and personally led the Indian delegation to the Conference of the Group of 77 on ECDC in Caracas, in May 1981. 1982 and 1983 were eventful years for India and its foreign policy. In the shadow of the Gulf war the Nonaligned Movement asked India to host the Seventh Summit. This also meant India assuming the Chair of the Movement and Smt. Indira Gandhi becomes its Chairperson. Shri P.V. Narasimha Rao presided over meetings of Foreign Ministers of Non-aligned Nations on the eve of the New Delhi Summit and also at the United Nations both in 1982, when India was asked to host the Summit and the following year when, at the initiative of the Movement, informal consultations amongst Heads of State and Government from diverse nations across the world were held at New York.

Shri Rao was also the Leader of the Special Non-aligned Mission that visited countries in West Asia in November 1983, in an effort to resolve the Palestian Liberation Organisation. Shri Rao was associated actively with the Commonwealth Heads of Government in New Delhi and with the Action Group set up by the meeting on the question of Cyprus. In his capacity as Minister of External Affairs, Shri Narasimha Rao has chaired on behalf of India a number of Joint Commissions including those with the U.S.A., U.S.S.R., Pakistan, Bangladesh, Iran, Vietnam, Tanzania and Guyana.

Shri Narasimha Rao took over as Home Minister on July 19, 1984. He was re-appointed to this post, with the additional charge of the Ministry of Planning, on November 5, 1984. Appointed Minister of Defence from December 31, 1984 to September 25, 1985. On September 25, 1985 he took over as Minister of Human Resource Development.

Shri Narasimha Rao was the Prime Minister who introduced globalisation with a human face.

VII. Dr.N.T.Ramarao

Former Chief Minister of Andhra Pradesh

Shri NTR was born on 28 May 1923 tnkata Ramamma in Nimmakuru village in and Venkata Ramamma in Nimmakuru village in the Madras presidency of British India. After completing graduation from the Andhra Christian College in Guntur, Rao joined the Madras Service Commission as a sub-registrar. But his dreams lay somewhere else. He wanted to act. So he left his job in three weeks.He debuted in the Telugu film industry with Mana Desam in 1949.

Two years later, he broke through with Pathala Bharaivi (1951), an enduring classic in the Telugu film history. Over his three-decade-long career, NTR prominently worked in mythological films, playing characters from Vishnu to Shiva.

Remarkably, he played the role of Krishna in 17 films, a fact that perhaps helped him later in his political career. He played the role of Lord Krishna in Maya Bazaar (1957), Ravana in Bhookailasa (1958), Bhishma in Bhishma (1962), Lord Rama in Lava Kusa (1963), Arjuna in Nartanasala (1963) and the triple role of Krishna, Karna and Duryodhana in Daana Veera Soora Karna (1977). He continued to work in films till 1982 with immense success as an actor and producer. He also acted in over 300 films. He was awarded a Padma Shri for his contribution to Indian cinema in 1968. In 1982, he formed the TDP to rid the state of Congress rule and within a year, his party formed the first non-Congress government in the state. Two years later, Rao had to leave for abroad for a coronary bypass surgery. In his absence, Ram Lal, then governor of the state, appointed NTR's finance minister Nadendla Bhaskara as chief minister of the state. To regain his chair, NTR employed a strategy he had successfully used earlier for election campaigning — 'Chaitanya Rathan', a political chariot tour of the state. With a deepening political turmoil, the Indira Gandhi government reluctantly replaced Lal with Shankar Dayal Sharma, who appointed NTR as chief minister. A populist leader, NTR introduced the mid-day meal programme in schools and banned alcohol in the state, among other moves. His measures increased the popularity of his party, but the economy of the state suffered. He returned to power in 1994 in alliance with the Left parties, but was dislodged in a coup led by his son-in-law N. Chandrababu Naidu over a familial dispute that stemmed from fears that Rao's second wife was set to take over the party. In 1996, after a long career in public life, NTR died of cardiac arrest.

Late N.T.Rama Rao had shown special interest towards poor and introduced programmes like Rs,2 per Kg of rice and Janatha Saries to the poor.The Author's case is another example (a Scheduled Tribe). He invited the Author and made him the Vice-Chancellor of the erst while Jawaharlal Nehru Technological University (JNTU), Hyderabad when he was working as Joint Secretary in the University Grants Commission (UGC), New Delhi.

VIII. THE POPULAR PRIME MINISTER OF INDIA

Shri Narendra Modi

Shri Narendra Modi was sworn-in as India's Prime Minister on 30th May 2019, marking the start of his second term in office. The first ever Prime Minister to be born after Independence, Shri Modi has previously served as the Prime Minister of India from 2014 to 2019. He also has the distinction of being the longest serving Chief Minister of Gujarat with his term spanning from October 2001 to May 2014.He belogs to Bhartiya Janatha Party (BJP).

Inspired by the motto of 'Sabka Saath, Sabka Vikas, Sabka Vishwas', Shri Modi has ushered in a paradigm shift in governance that has led to inclusive, development-oriented and corruption-free governance. The Prime Minister has worked with speed and scale to realise the aim of Antyodaya, or ensuring last-mile delivery of schemes and services.

Leading international agencies have noted that under the leadership of PM Narendra Modi, India has been eliminating poverty at record pace. This is attributed to a series of pro-poor decisions taken by the Central Government.

Today, India is home to the world's largest healthcare programme, Ayushman Bharat. Covering over 50 crore Indians, Ayushman Bharat provides top quality and affordable healthcare to the poor and neo-middle class.

The Lancet, considered among the most prestigious health journals in the world has lauded Ayushman Bharat, stating that this scheme attends to the larger discontent about the health sector in India. The journal also noted PM Modi's efforts to prioritise universal health coverage.

Understanding that financial exclusion was a bane for the poor, the Prime Minister launched the Pradhan Mantri Jan Dhan Yojana that aimed at opening bank accounts for every Indian. Now, over 35 crore Jan Dhan accounts have been opened. These accounts have not only banked the unbanked but also opened the doors for other avenues of empowerment.

Going a step ahead of Jan Dhan, Shri Modi emphasised on Jan Suraksha, by giving insurance and pension cover to the most vulnerable sections of society. The JAM trinity (Jan Dhan- Aadhaar- Mobile) has led to elimination of middle men and ensured transparency and speed, powered by technology.

In a first, over 42 crore people associated with the unorganised sector now have pension coverage under the Pradhan Mantri Shram Yogi Man Dhan Yojana. During the very first Cabinet Meeting after the 2019 election results, a similar pension scheme for traders was announced as well.

The Pradhan Mantri Ujjwala Yojana, launched in 2016 provides free cooking gas connections to the poor. It has proven to be a major game-changer in providing smoke-free kitchens to over 7 crore beneficiaries, most of whom are women.18,000 villages that were without electricity even after 70 long years of Independence have been electrified.

Shri Modi believes that no Indian should be homeless and to realise this vision, over 1.25 crore houses were built between 2014 and 2019. The pace of house construction remains as quick to fulfil the PM's vision of 'Housing for All' by 2022.Shri Modi has also focused path-breaking initiatives for agriculture ranging from Soil Health Cards, E-NAM for better markets and a renewed focus on irrigation. On 30th May 2019, PM Modi fulfilled a major promise by creating a new Jal Shakti Ministry to cater to all aspects relating to water resources. On 2nd October 2014, Mahatma Gandhi's Birth Anniversary, the PM launched 'Swachh Bharat Mission' a mass movement for cleanliness across the nation. The scale and impact of the movement is historic. Today, sanitation coverage has risen from 38% in 2014 to 99%. Several states and Union Territories have been declared open defecation free (ODF). Substantive measures been taken for a clean Ganga. The World Health Organisation has appreciated the Swachh Bharat Mission and has opined that it would save three lakh lives.PM Modi launched the 'Make in India' initiative to turn India into an international manufacturing powerhouse. This effort has led to transformative results. For instance, the number of mobile manufacturing units has risen from 2 in 2014 to 122 in 2019. India has made significant strides in 'Ease of Doing Business', improving its ranking from 142 in 2014 to 77 in 2019. The Government of India rolled out the GST during a historic session of Parliament in 2017, which has realised the dream of 'One Nation, One Tax.'During his tenure, special attention has been paid to India's rich history and culture. India is home to the world's largest statue, the State of Unity, a fitting tribute to Sardar Patel. This Statue was built through a special mass movement where tools of farmers and soil from all states and Union Territories of India were used, signifying the spirit of 'Ek Bharat, Shreshtha Bharat.'Going a step ahead of climate change, PM Modi has talked about climate justice. In 2018, Heads of State and Government from several nations came to India for the launch of the International Solar Alliance, an innovative effort to harness solar energy for a better planet.Recognising his efforts towards environmental conservation, PM Modi was honoured with the United Nations 'Champions of the Earth Award.' Narendra Modi's clarion call for marking a day as 'International Day of Yoga' received an overwhelming response at the UN. In a first, a total of 177 Nations across the world came together and passed the resolution to declare 21st June as the 'International Day of Yoga at the UN.'Shri Modi was born on 17 September, 1950, in a small town in Gujarat. His family belonged to the 'other backward class' which is among the marginalised sections of society. He grew up in a poor but loving family 'without a spare rupee'. The initial hardships of life not only taught the value of hard work but also exposed him to the avoidable sufferings of the common people. This inspired him from a very young age to immerse himself in service of people and the nation. In his initial years, he worked with the Rashtriya Swayamsevak Sangh (RSS), a nationalist organisation devoted to nation building and later devoted himself in politics working with the Bharatiya Janata Party organization at National and State level. Shri Modi completed his MA in political science from Gujarat University.

Narendra Modi is a 'People's Leader', dedicated to solving their problems and improving their well-being. Nothing is more satisfying to him than being amongst the people, sharing their joys and alleviating their sorrows. His powerful 'personal connect' with the people on ground is complemented by a strong online presence. He is known as India's most techno-savvy leader, using the web to reach people and bring about change in their lives. He is very active on social media platforms including Face book, Twitter, Instegram, Sound Cloud, Linkedin, Weibo and other forums.Beyond politics, Narendra Modi enjoys writing. He has authored several books, including poetry. He begins his day with Yoga, which strengthens his body and mind and instills the power of calmness in an otherwise fast-paced routine.

CHAPTER-VIII
EMPOWERMENT OF SOCIALLY DISADVANTAGED GROUPS

Social empowerment relates to the empowerment of socially disadvantaged groups, namely viz., the scheduled caste, the scheduled tribes, the other backward classes,minorities, and women and children. The cases of disabled, aged and infirm and social deviants could also be included in this category. Their share in the country's total population is quite substantial. Thus, the empowerment of the socially disadvantaged groups assumes importance. Education is a means to achieve this.

Social Empowerment cannot be viewed in isolation. It is influenced by economic empowerment and political empowerment as well. Therefore, while considering social empowerment, we have to consider economic empowerment and political empowerment also.

EDUCATION AND SOCIAL EMPOWERMENT

I. INTRODUCTION

Statement made in the resolution of the Government of India while appointing the committee to review the National Policy on Education (NPE), 1986 rightly summarised the education scenario in the country.

It states: "Despite efforts at social and economic development since the attainment of independence, a majority of our people continue to remain deprived of education. It is also a matter of grave concern that our people comprise 50 per cent of the world's illiterates and large sections of children have to go without an acceptable level of primary education. Government accords the highest priority to education both as a human right and as the means for bringing about a transformation towards a more humane and enlightened society. There is a need to make education an effective instrument for securing equality for women and persons belonging to the backward classes and minorities.

Moreover, it is essential to give work and employment orientation to education and exclude from it the elitist aberrations that have become a glaring characteristic of the educational scene. Educational institutions are increasingly being influenced by casteism, communalism, and obscurantism. It is necessary to emphasise struggle against this phenomenon and move towards a genuinely egalitarian and secular social order". There do not seem to be much independence in this educational scenario even today.

Education should contribute to the solutions of national problems like food sufficiency to the people through achieving self-sufficiency in food; economic growth and employment; safe drinking water, health and nutrition; housing, communications and transport; poverty alleviation; social and national integration; political development and improvement of the quality of life of the people.

Education should serve as the main instrument of change and be a vital component of human resources development. It should relate to the life, needs and aspirations of the people. It should be a vehicle for teaching social, moral and spiritual values, broadening mental horizons, and building good character and moral strength in man or women. The Slogan 'Education for All' should fructify in action. At the same time, we have to realise that "Quality Education for all is more important than education to all".

Social empowerment relates to the empowerment of socially disadvantaged groups, namely viz., the scheduled caste, the scheduled tribes, the other backward classes of minorities, and women and children. The cases of disabled, aged and infirm and social deviants could also be included in this category. The socially disadvantaged groups still lag behind society due to their social and economic backwardness. Their share in the country's total population is quite substantial. Thus, the empowerment of the socially disadvantaged groups assumes importance. Education is a means to achieve this.

Social Empowerment cannot be viewed in isolation. It is influenced by economic empowerment and political empowerment as well. Therefore, while considering social empowerment, we have to consider economic empowerment and political empowerment also.

TRIBAL EDUCATION

Several constitutional provisions exist for the protection and promotion of the interests of the scheduled tribes. In conformity with the directive principles of state policy, social justice has been an avowed goal of development. During the past six decades, a variety of programmes have been launched by the government to improve the socio-economic conditions of the scheduled tribes. These measures, no doubt, yielded results but not commensurate with the efforts or the needs of the target groups of scheduled tribes. Many scheduled tribes continue to be socially and educationally backwards and languish at the bottom of the social and economic pyramid. Education is paramount for the social, economic and political empowerment of tribals.

GENERAL OBSERVATIONS

1. High incidence of illiteracy, especially among the female population and primitive tribal groups.

2. Need for the medium of instruction in tribal dialects.

3. The heavy dropout rate of nearly 80% in primary education.

4. Lack of commitment on the part of teachers.

5. Need for the participation of the local community in educational activities.

6. Lack of suitable infrastructure facilities.

7. Need for proper orientation of teachers and other administrators about tribal life and culture.

8. Inadequate and untimely supply of textbooks and notebooks and insufficient provision of incentives.

9. Lack of proper medical aid and balanced diet to the tribal students.

10. Lack of monitoring mechanism to motivate dropout tribal students for continuation of education.

11. Lack of suitable self-employment opportunities to the educated youth and dropouts.

STRATEGIES

1. The N.C.E.R.T. and S.C.E.R.T., Non-governmental Organisations (N.G.O's) have to prepare and induce bi-lingual textbooks in the first two standards where ever that particular dialect is the mother tongue of a minimum 1 lakh population. N.C.E.R.T. should be made responsible for introducing textbooks in all the states and union territories of the country.

2. As each region of tribal areas follows its ritual and agricultural calendar, the concerned tribal research institutes have to prepare these calendars either region-wise or tribe-wise and furnish the same to the education department for taking necessary action.

3. The National Institutes like N.C.E.R.T., N.E.P.A. and state institutions like S.C.E.R.T., TRIs have to organise orientation courses and workshops for the tribal areas regularly.

4. The concerned state governments should provide the necessary infrastructural facilities such as permanent buildings, playgrounds, suitable audio-video aids including Television, Radio, Tape-recorders etc. At least a group of schools may be provided with these facilities, which five schools can share in the particular area.

5. The Medical officers in charge of the Primary Health Centers or Mobile Medical Units have to visit each educational Institution at least once a fortnight for regular medical check-ups. The medical department may give suitable instructions to these Primary Health Centers. The tribal welfare departments have to provide transportation facilities to the doctors to visit these schools wherever the P.H.Centers do not have medical centers. Tribal

welfare department should get the menu-cards for each residential institution including ashram schools in consultation with National Institute of Nutrition. While preparing the Menu-cards locally available food material and culinary habits of the local tribals have to be considered.

6. Teaching-aids have to be prepared based on local culture and environment. Local tribal folk dances, and music-both vocal and instrumental, should be included in the curricular and co-curricular activities.

7. Progress cards are a must in the educational institutions. Below average students have to be identified and extra-coaching should be provided.

8. The concerned district authorities have to monitor the progress made in these directions.

9. Adult and non-formal education should be compulsorily introduced (gender-based) in tribal villages. The reading material should be prepared with tribal bias. The gaps in the Literacy levels between scheduled tribes and the general population should be bridged.

10. Each educational institution has to send monthly progress reports indicating results of weakly/monthly tests, syllabus covered, health conditions of the inmates etc. These formats have to be formulated by the tribal welfare department and ciruclated to all institutions. Project officers/D.E.O's have to take special care of these educational institutions and send progress reports to the concerned heads of the departments.

11. N.G.O.'s have to be involved in the promotion of education and literacy among the Scheduled Tribes. Each N.G.O. should adopt minimum five educational institutions and render assistance like clothes, and medical aid for deserving students. They should act as surrogate parents in extending love and affection to the kids.

12. Expert teams may be constituted by involving educationists, experts, anthropologists and these teams should visit the institutions which are getting poor results in the common examinations. These teams have to suggest concerning authorities including governments, remedial action to be taken for improving the quality of education. Residential School Authorities/Tribal Departments have to constitute these teams.

13. In order to promote literacy and education to boys and girls belonging to S.Ts have to be provided additional incentives like 2 extra-pairs of clothes, school bag, chappals and to and fro-fares. The concerned I.T.D.A.'s must take up the responsibility and government of India, ministry of social justice and empowerment have to provide required funds to all the concerned states and union territories.

EDUCATION OF DALITS

OBSERVATIONS & RECOMMENDATIONS

1. There is need for mass publicity of the preamble of the Indian Constitution

2. 'Annihilation of Castes' a book written by Dr.B.R.Ambedkar may be prescribed as one of the textbooks in the post metric studies.

3. Drastic steps are to be introduced to curb the social evil of untouchability

4. Compulsory free education should be provided to girl child belonging to dalits and other weaker sections.

5. The upper ceiling limit on income of parents of S.Cs and S.Ts students may be fixed at Rs 50,000/- for availing educational privileges and scholarships.

6. Filling up of all backlog vacancies of SC's and ST's in Central Government and different states should be under taken within a stipulated time frame.

7. Training Programmes should be offered to enable interested Dalits to start small   scale industries.

8. Special drive may be undertaken to enroll cent percent SC school going children. Special coaching for low achievers should be organised.

9. Inequalities among SC's need to be recognised and programmes should be introduced to improve the educational levels of lower strata among the SCs.

10. Government should publish a separate booklet containing all the educational facilities available for SC students. These booklets and other material should be made available in all the educational institutions.

11. Vocational training courses for dalits should be introduced in High schools in order to impart skills to students who can earn their livelihood while studying.

12. Government should step up its financial support for higher education and also subsidise cost of higher education to weaker sections.

13. The Autonomous Colleges should also contribute their share for promotion of educational development of Dalits.

14. Some of the Residential Schools established for promotion of education mainly among SC's are not working well. There is a need to streamline the functioning of these Residential Schools which are mainly established to impart quality education.

STRATEGIES

1. Preamble of the Indian Constitution should become a part of the curriculum in the textbooks at all levels of Educational Institutions. As the preamble contains quintessence of the Constitution and also goals of social justice, it should be translated in to regional Languages. Publicity could also be given in the electronic media.

2. All the State Governments may get Dr. B.R. Ambedkar's book "Annihilation of castes" translated into the regional languages, and prescribe it as a non-detailed book.

3. The N.G.O's which are committed to the cause of dalits are to be entrusted with the responsibility of creating proper awareness in the rural areas where the problem of untouchability is acute. The political leadership and other social workers should lead the movements wherever there are problems of prohibition of temple entry to the scheduled castes. Social welfare department should prepare an action plan in this regard.

4. After verifying the success of the education guarantee scheme (E.G.S) being implemented in the rural areas of Madhya Pradesh, similar schemes may be formulated by Social welfare departments for the benefit of S.C.s and other weaker sections.

5. As there are thousands of backlog of vacancies reserved for S.Cs and S.T.s. State governments and the Central government may draw up crash programmes to fill up these vacancies.

6. The Education Departments, at state level may launch a scheme by which in the educational institutions both technical and non-technical, low achievers belonging to SCs could be identified and special coaching could be arranged.

7. As there are wide disparities in the educational levels of sub-castes among scheduled castes, special or exclusive residential schools should be started for such groups. Social welfare departments should identify low literacy areas and implement these educational programmes.

8. The social welfare department should take up the responsibility of the preparation of detailed booklets containing all the educational facilities starting from primary school level to post-doctoral courses and make these booklets available not only in educational institutions but also in gram panchayats and other service organisations.

9. Appropriate vocational courses may be started in the present residential high schools and junior colleges for the benefit of SC and ST students.

10. Social welfare departments have to reimburse the total cost of education of SCs including technical and professional education. They should meet not only the cost of the books but also other expenses including proper clothing and transportation.

11. The A.P.S.W. Residential Institutions Society should identify those Residential Schools, which are not achieving good results commensurate with their investments. This Organisation should take up immediate measures for rectifying the situation.

EDUCATIONAL DEVELOPMENT OF MINORITIES

Muslims are the largest minorities in the country and are unevenly spread. Economically, educational-wise and psychologically they are oppressed. Minorities are not properly represented in political field. Among the minorities, again Buddhists and Christians are provided with good education whereas it is not the case with Muslims and Jains.

In Madarsas not only the Urdu language but also science and maths are taught to the students. Bridge courses and summer schools should be encouraged. Adoption to area approach to identify areas and mandals should be considered. Teaching learning materials should be provided and crash programmes should be organised in those identified areas. Construction of girls hostels and ashram schools will encourage the minority girl child education. NGO's should be come forward in each district to focus on minority issues. Culture of minority groups should have space in textbooks. Promotion of national integration through educational institutions, Instructions in minority language and refresher courses for teachers should be arranged.

Poor economic status will not facilitate providing good education for Muslim Minorities especially due to privatisation of education. They cannot afford to have education or afford to buy books. This backwardness, lack of education makes them to stand where they are. There is no progress and there are only a few Urdu medium schools. There are no avenues at higher education level. Unemployment problem is severe. Badly they are in need of learning Urdu language. In Madarsas there is no provision for modern education. Scholarships are to be provided. More centers are required for coaching in A.P.

The problem of Muslim woman is particularly acute than with others. The problems of educational opportunities and her observing purdah system does not allow her to expose to society. She should come to the main stream of life and fight for her liberty, equality and fraternity. Muslim women are still in dilemma whether to follow religious based personal law or uniform civil code. To understand and enlighten themselves they require education and they must come to the mainstream of life.

The contribution of Christians to the educational development in India is considerable. The original motivation for the introduction of western education has undergone changes through time. Post independent India saw these institutions come under constrain of article 30. Today new challenges face these institutions. They have to read their priorities and work under the pressure of government interference. Yet they are still doing fruitful work.

More concrete and positive efforts are need for the educational development and welfare of Minorities.

EDUCATION OF BACKWARD CLASSES

The Backward classes form a major chunk of the Indian population. The constitution specially recognised their existence as a category of people called the socially and educationally Backward Classes or Backward Classes other than the Scheduled Castes & Scheduled Tribes. The constitution also recognised that they labour under difficulties and envisaged the appointment of a Commission by the President of India under article 340 of the Constitution.

Every effort must be made for the educational development of the Backward Classes and to bring about parity at all levels with others. The following measures will contribute towards this objective:

1. Training for the up gradation of the skills of the artisans and introduction of modern technology in their crafts should be undertaken, if necessary, through an Institutional basis.

2. Economic empowerment of women should be improved through imparting additional skills

3. Food for Education for More and Most Backward Classes children of school-going age should be taken up on a nationwide basis;

4. Every good professional institution in the District/State/Country, whether public or private, in the same proportion as the percentage of reservation in education for them existing from time to time and should be educated there up to the level of their choice. The Government should meet the full cost of the education and maintenance of each such student in accordance with the actual cost of the education in each such institution, and boarding and lodging expenses in a hostel attached to such institutions or, in

the absence of such attached hostel, in other appropriate hostel and should also meet any other financial costs by whatever name known, wherever charged;

5. One residential school each for boys and girls of backward classes should be set up in each district on the pattern existing in Andhra Pradesh, with 75% of the seats going to the candidates of the BCs of the specific category of weaker sections and the remaining 25% for the candidates belonging to SCs and STs and to the candidates of general categories. This facility should be provided in private residential schools also in view of the large number of private institutions of general as well as specified education at all levels set up in the past and that may be set up in future, and the advantage that the candidates passing out of such institutions have. In districts where a residential schools for Backward Classes is not immediately possible, there should be a hostel one each for BC Boys and BC Girls which can later be expanded into a residential school.

6. Selection grade posts of teachers should be created and selection grade teachers should be appointed only in these residential schools and similar residential schools for other weaker sections.

7. In view of the fact that a sizeable number of students have qualified and increasing numbers will in future qualify from educational institutions of general as well as specialized/professional education in foreign countries, and the career advantage those candidates passing out from foreign institutions have in the country, the Government should send, at its cost, fully covering fees and other mandatory payments, maintenance and travel cost, Backward Class candidates in the same proportion in relation to the general

category candidates who go to such institutions on their own or otherwise, as the percentage of reservation in education fixed for them from time to time, to good institutions in each such country in every area of education, every year.

8. The selection of Backward Class candidates for purposes like admission to residential schools and colleges and universities, public as well as private, Indian as well as foreign, should be made on merit among them through competitive examinations with suitable weightage for candidates from More and Most Backward Classes.

9. Provision of scholarships scheme for research scholars at Ph.D. and higher levels and enhancing the level of scholarship amount to realistically high level so that the academic and intellectual potential among the Backward Classes may have the full scope for realisation.

10. In all these measures, there should be special focused attention on More and Most backward classes and girls.

EDUCATION OF WOMEN

Women account for nearly 50% of the Indian population. Indian Society being conservative for ages with male domination, women have been the oppressed lot and at least in the modern democratic India they should have received a better deal with equal status, opportunities and dignity. However efforts and achievements in this regard are grossly inadequate during the past fifty and odd years of our Independence.

India has ratified various international conventions and human rights instruments committing to secure equal rights for women.

Key among them is the ratification of Convention on the Elimination of all forms of Discrimination against Women (CEDAW-1979) in 1993. The Mexico Plan of Action (1975), the Nairobi Forward Looking Strategies (1985), the Beijing Declaration as well as the platform for Action (1995) have been unreservedly endorsed by India for appropriate follow up.

However, there still exists a very wide gap between the goals enunciated in the constitution, legislation, policies, plans, programmes and related mechanisms, on the one hand and the situational reality of the status of women in India, on the other. This has been analysed extensively in the Report of the Committee on the Status of Women in India, "Towards Equality" (1974), and highlighted in the National Perspective Plan for Women (1988-2000) and the "Shramshakti Report (1988).

There has been a significant shift in the approach towards well being of women from 'Welfare during Fifties' to 'Development during Seventies' and to 'Empowerment during Nineties'.

The Need of education for women should be emphasized as a "Strategic imperative" to assert and maintain their dignity and self-respect on par with men. The factors responsible for the high percentage of illiteracy among women as well as the high drop-out rate among girl students at primary, middle and secondary school levels should be analysed. A critical review of the various programmes like DPEP, Lok Jumbish, Shikshakarmi etc present their unsatisfactory impact on controlling the drop-out rate among school-going girls. In contrast to this negative aspect of women's education at the school level, it may be pointed out that there were hopeful signs on higher, vocational and technical education as reflected in the increasing number of women enrolling in such courses. Women's participation in higher, vocational and technical education which was only 0.34+ percent in 1950-51 increased to 13.1 percent in 1995-96. The high drop-out rate at primary and secondary levels was due to various reasons including non-existence of schools within the reach of the homes of girls, dearth of female teachers, increasing cost of education and lack of motivation on the part of parents who consider a girl child as "Paraya dhan". In order to address this problem successfully women themselves should evolve and adopt goal oriented sound strategies. The contribution of village level education committees and economic empowerment of women would go a long way in facilitating the spread of education among women at different levels.

It may be stressed that special attention should be paid to the already identified low female literacy pockets, and to women and girl-children belonging to the socially disadvantaged groups. Special efforts should be made to ensure easy and equal access to education for women and girls through commitment to achieve total eradication of illiteracy.

Universal compulsory and free primary education and a strategy to spread literacy among women should be undertaken. Vocationalisation of secondary education and vocational training for women as a means of empowering women to become economically self-reliant. The Central Government should raise the outlay on education to 6.5% of GDP from the current 3.0%.

There is discrimination between the education of boys and that of girls with the former being preferred to the latter. The deplorable low educational status of Dalit women engendered by an abject poverty compels parents to send their children to work in order to supplement the meagre earnings of the family. Without educating women it would be futile to attempt to abolish social evils like dowry, ill-treatment of women, etc. Education is an absolute need in order to enable women to assert their basic rights as human being and enjoy a dignified and respectable status in society.

It is woman who creates and sustains values in the society. As such education is a prerequisite for women to keep society value-orientated, altruistic and spiritual.

The role of education in the personality development of woman and her empowerment for effective participation in nation-building as well as to fight for the liberation of women from social injustice and economic slavery which are responsible for the miserable plight of women at present needs no emphasis. Education of women should be more holistic and geared to the special needs of women. The content of women's education should be determined in terms of equipping women with knowledge and skills to play their legitimate role in society and contribute to the total well-being of the nation. Women should not be treated as mere custodians of traditional society into all its archaic values and customs but as persons having potentialities to enter any arena of life and practice any profession. In order to empower women to participate effectively in politics and the democratic decision-making process the government should take effective steps to pass necessary legislation providing for reservation of seats in the parliament and state legislatures for women.

The economic dominance of men is the main cause of the low status of women in society. Unless women were made economically self-reliant their conditions would not improve. Men and women should be jointly responsible for maintaining the family and share equally in domestic activities.

The approach towards Women's development and the scope for their participation in the national development should be more refined.

Some of the following efforts are needed in this regard:

1. An integrated approach should be adopted towards empowering women; this underscores harmonisation of various efforts on different fronts viz., social, economic, legal and political.

2. Gender Justice remained a distant goal as more than two hundred million women are still illiterate in the country. So, efforts should be made to fulfill the goal of "education for Women's equality" as laid down in the revised National Policy on Education (NPE), 1992.

3. For Capacity Building of Women, attention should be paid to their health, especially the reproduction health and their access to health care services. A life cycle approach to Women's health should be adopted.

4. Economic empowerment of women based on their participation in the decision making process with regard to incomes, investments and expenditure at all levels, should receive utmost attention.

5. Considering the strong impact environmental factors have on the sustenance and livelihood of women, participation of women should be ensured in conservation of environment and control of environmental degradation.

6. The media policy should include a component by which it becomes an instrument in projecting a positive image of women. Strict ban on the depiction of demeaning, degrading, negative and conventional image of women and violence against women should be enforced through legislation, regulatory mechanisms and media policies.

7. Education is the Key for the empowerment of women. So highest priority should be given to raise the percentage of literacy among women, which is very low at present. To this end, the constitutional provision regarding universal free and compulsory primary education should be implemented immediately. Further women should be entitled to receive free education at all stages-primary, secondary and higher. In order to check the drop-out rate among girl-children, financial compensation should be given to their parents who are compelled by poverty to send their girls to work in fields and factories to supplement their family earnings.

8. High priority should be given to the vocationalisation of women's education and vocational training for women. This is absolutely necessary to enable women to become economically independent and self-reliant. Adequate opportunities and encouragement should be given to women to pursue professional courses in engineering and medical colleges and other technical institutes.

9. The present curricula and courses of study followed in educational institutions at various levels are too formal and theoretical and male-oriented to meet the special needs and

aspirations of women, and equip them with knowledge and skills needed to solve their problems. So efforts are needed to make women's education more comprehensive and holistic so that it would deal with the specific and special challenges and problems facing women today.

CHILDREN

A Country's future depends on their Children, Children's attitudes, habits, health, education, appreciation and inculcation of human values and Country's ethos have a direct bearing on having a healthy society and a peaceful, stable and strong nation in the future.

Education has become a nightmare for children with heavily loaded syllabus, books, homework, coping with additional preparation for competition and so on. It is curbing their creativity and sensitivities for finer things of life. They need time and facilities for recreation, sports, cultural activities, creative activities and adventure.

The problem of child labour, child abuses and street children are the curse on the society. The Girl child has peculiar problems of its own. The contemporary media has also unwanted effect on the young minds.

Children's rights need focus. Disabled children have special problems. Children who are orphaned due to communal disturbances, terrorism and other calamities need rehabilitation for their future.

The following measures need attention for the development of children:

1. Though the living conditions of children have improved, still there is a long way to go before all children in our country

will have adequate opportunities to enjoy their childhood and develop into responsible citizens capable of making their legitimate contribution to the development of the Nation. This is a matter of concern for all "Right Thinking" people in order to meet the challenges of child development.

2.   Education is the most important factor of child development but millions of children are not able to get even primary education; consequently they are forced to work in hazardous jobs. They are also denied their fundamental right to grow as healthy and responsible citizens. So, in order to enable every child to realise and develop his all-round personality should be given an opportunity to go to school and get good education.

3.   In order to facilitate children from poor families to attend school the mid-day meal scheme must be introduced and implemented strictly. In the case of dropout child it is necessary to open Non-formal and vocational schools where they can pick up literacy as well as learn certain vocational skills and become self employed.

4.   The present education in schools is not helping students in their character formation. Since it is overweighed in favour of knowledge, information and skills formation it ignores the moral and spiritual development of the students. This imbalance needs to be corrected by introducing value education based on the rich spiritual and cultural heritage of India, values of the freedom struggle, the constitutional values and the lives of great men and women.

5. As a consequence of revolutionary development in the field of Information and communication technology the children are exposed to many negative influences. The aggressive and violent tendencies noticed in the behavior of children to some extent can be attributed to the negative influences of press and electronic Media. The culture of violence, sex and other evil forces is by and large the result of such evil influences. In order to counteract this negative influence of the media it is necessary that parents and teachers should guide the Children in the choice of programmes over the T.V, internet, as well as the reading of novels and seeing films.

6. Special attention should be given to the disabilities and their prevention and discrimination to the which girl child is subjected to in the society at large and to facilitate the girl child in the family, in the school and in the society to enjoy her rights and develop as equal, independent and responsible human being. The Government as well as civil society should evolve suitable programmes for education, employment, personality development and other cultural development.

7. There are several millions of physically handicapped and mentally retarded children who are at present not properly cared for either by the society or Government. Their life should be made happy and enjoyable. More homes for the disabled and mentally retarded should be established in proper environment and adequate facilities for their growth as responsible human beings capable of living independently with dignity and self-respect, should be provided.

8.   The children's growth is handicapped because of overcrowded classrooms, and overburdened syllabus and textbooks. This tyranny inflected on the students by the schools should come to an end. Educationists and policy makers should take appropriate steps to reduce this burden and make study a happy and enjoyable pursuit.

9.   It is noted that several children are maimed or become orphans in times of war and terrorist activity. Many children lose their parents because of the explosion of mines planted by terrorists and therefore it is necessary to enact strict laws to prevent such situations and such children's burden should become the first charge on the society.

SOCIALLY DISABLED

POLITICAL EMPOWERMENT

The socially disadvantaged groups still lag behind the rest of the society due to their social and economic backwardness. Their share in the country's total population is quiet substantial. Thus, the empowerment of the socially disadvantaged groups assumes importance.

Political Empowerment is an important tool to achieve social empowerment of the socially disabled.

REVIEW

The consultation paper on pace of socio-economic change under the constitution brought out by National Commission to Review the Working of the Constitution (May, 2001) points out that despite manifest, avowed and determined concern of the Constitution for

uplift and welfare of the Scheduled Castes, Scheduled Tribes and Backward Classes, the objectives have not been achieved. Whatever has been done in this regard has been done hesitatingly, half-heartedly and as a measure of concession forgetting that this relates to their Constitutional rights and not concession to those classes. Supported by relevant statistics the following observations are made, in the paper, in respect of the Scheduled Castes, Scheduled Tribes and backward classes.

1. The high number of cases registered under the Protection of Civil Rights Act, 1955 and the Scheduled Castes and the Scheduled Tribes (Prevention of Atrocities) Act, 1989 shows that atrocities against Scheduled Castes and the Scheduled Tribes and untouchability continue unabated even today.

2. Representation of Scheduled Castes and Scheduled Tribes in Group 'B' & Group 'A' posts in Central Government itself continues to remain inadequate and Scheduled Tribes are not even adequately represented in Group 'C' and Group 'D' services.

3. The paper notes that the reservation for other backward communities in Central services was provided only in 1990 and became operational from 1993 onwards and sufficient statistical data are not yet available to draw any definite conclusions to the extent, their reservation has improved in the central services but the adequate representation of backward classes in public services is, still a far cry.

4. Landlessness is increasing amongst the Scheduled Castes and the proportion of the Scheduled Caste agricultural labourers to

the Scheduled Caste cultivators is increasing which indicates that the Scheduled Caste cultivators after losing their land holdings are becoming agricultural labourers. The results are not very different for Scheduled Tribes also.

5. Some studies, the paper notes, have pointed out that allocation of funds for the development and welfare of the Scheduled Castes and Scheduled Tribes has shown a steadily declining trend since the late eighties.

6. Allocations for welfare of the Scheduled Castes, the Scheduled Tribes and backward classes do not match their developmental needs and priorities and implementation of schemes makes the matter worse.

POLITICAL EMPOWERMENT

The consultation paper on Pace of Socio-economic change under the Constitution of the National Commission to Review the Working of the Constitution notes that the full potential of women remains grossly underutilized even after more than 51 years of the working of the Constitution and suggests steps to enhance the representation of women at various levels of policy making and administration and for the process of empowerment of women that began with reservation of one-third seats in Panchayats and municipalities to State Legislatures and Parliament.

Clearance of the pending Bill in the Parliament regarding women's reservation in Parliament and State Assemblies will add in a big measure to the empowerment of women.

LOCAL SELF-GOVERNMENT OF TRIBAL AREAS

ISSUES

1. Lack of elected representatives of gram Panchayats situated in Tribal Areas/Scheduled Areas.

2. Inadequate financial resources & income to gram panchayats.

3. Delay in releasing of funds to gram panchayats by government

4. Proliferation of various Institutions at village level such as VTDA (Village Tribal Development Agency). VSS (Vana Rakshana Samitis) and other committees of Janma Bhoomi.

5. Lack of co-ordination among various agencies at District, Mandal and Village level.

6. Interference of ITDA in functioning of Panchayat Raj Institutions at village level resulting in weakening of initiative of Local elected members.

7. Various committees constituted under Janma Bhoomi are detrimental to the functioning of grama sabha, as per the provisions of the 73rd constitutional amendment.

STRATEGIES

1. Elections have to be conducted immediately as per the provisions of amended panchayat raj act in the light of the 73rd constitution amendment. The concerned government has to take initiative and complete elections in stipulated time-period.

2. The provisions of the grama sabhas as per the constitutional amendment, and amended panchayat raj act have to be translated

into local tribal dialects and should be made available to all the gram panchayats situated in scheduled areas.

3. All the grama sabha members including tribal women should be enlightened about the functions, responsibilities & powers of the New gram sabhas that are being constituted. Regular peripatetic training programmes have to be organised in every gram panchayat and all the members have to be informed about the powers, and responsibilities of the gramsabha. Charts, booklets, posters, have to be prepared in regional and as well as in tribal dialect, highlighting the important provisions of the acts, including powers of gram sabha and the reading material should be made available at all gram sabha- panchayats & tribal areas.

4. The relevant portions of New Panchayat Raj Act & Gram Sabha, should be included in the syllabi of the reading material of Adult-Literacy centers, functional literacy/Non-formal educational centers.

5. Tribal women-folk have to be specially trained to take up the responsibilities as envisaged in the New gram sabha. They should be also being enlightened about various regulations pertaining to protective regulations.

The officials at the ITDA level and Mandal and village level should also be oriented about the new provisions, so as to facilitate them to take up all **kinds of developmental activities with the consent of gram sabha.**

Government has to issue orders to all departments, not to take up any kind of work without the consent of the concerned gram sabha.

All other Institutions at the village level should be brought under the control of gram sabha only in tribal areas.

SOCIO AND POLITICAL DEVELOPMENT OF MINORITIES

It is generally felt that no benefit has acquired to the Muslims for various Government Schemes, aimed at improving the conditions of disadvantaged sections of the society. This has supplemented by data on houses allotted to the middle income groups, licenses issued for fair price shops, benefit extended to the artisans by the Khadi and Village Industries Commissioner in a Seminar on Minorities.

He has argued that the Indian Minorities have been discriminated in the economic field. He has supplemented his argument with data.

He has pointed out that there is only marginal representation of Muslims in the services.

To improve the situations of Muslimshe the following steps are suggested:

Establishment of Muslim chamber of commerce

Establishment of Separate Ministry at the Centre for the Welfare of Muslims minorities.

Activate the Minority Financial Corporation in every state.

Reactivate the scheme of coaching run by Muslim Voluntary Organisations under Social Welfare Department

Muslims should establish their own co-operative banks, particularly in rural areas to improve the plight of rural Muslims.

Opening of centers for HRD among Muslims at each district and improve the plight of rural Muslims.

It is suggested to consider further the following steps for social and political development of minorities:

Imparting of education to these sections of the people,

Social participation.

Change in the customs.

Change in the treatment of behavior in the society on par with others.

To impart commercial skills to the enterprising sections of the minorities.

To remove stigma of shyness and active participation with others.

Interaction with society and active participation with others.

Participation in the Legislatures, executive and judiciary.

Imparting training to take up vocational courses, free of cost even up to Ph.D. levels should be considered.

Construction of modern houses free of cost with all infrastructures with emphasis on clean and green environment may be a good suggestion.

A Monitoring committee may costituted to implement the above suggestions. The committee should comprise of local MLAs/MLCs, ZP Officials and chairman, the District Collector, Police authorities like DSPs, and representatives of the communities. It should interact with the society on various developmental activities so that they can also exchange and share their views and join the mainstream of the society by having monthly meetings.

It is the responsibility of the society, i.e. Government to see that the minorities also take active part in politics and developmental activities of the society. It should be guaranteed as a right. The implementation should be effective and result oriented and within the time limit of 5 years.

A separate Finance Advisory Committee in all the States with the representatives of the minorities exclusively creating funds for the development of minorities in all walks of life is needed.

Implementation and review committees are also needed to be formulated to monitor all developmental activities of this neglected lot.

Advertisement of Right to information committees are also to be formulated to remove the exploitation and age old customs beliefs, shyness, and to create access to the very informed society through inter caste marriages etc.

Land is the gift of the nature and is the legitimate right to its subjects/people to cultivate/irrigate to get good yields, to practice the eminence of other human beings in the world, latest information. Nature has an in-built quality of giving equal opportunity to its living beings (human beings) but still the inequality is prevailing even after 50 years of independence. Proportionate land distribution is now required to see that everybody gets their share of the Nature at least in future or else the baby that is born may feel shy of its birth on the earth. Inequalities are the main cause for the backwardness of our country. This has to be overcome by formulated schemes/programmes afresh to reach the progress and development especially economy of the each person/citizen of the nation.

The sons of the soil separated merely on the grounds of religion should not be a hindrance among the minorities.

They have to come together, to demonstrate their unity and solidarity to seize political power, which will solve all problems.

Initiate a dialogue with the Hindu organisations with objective of minimizing and ultimately eliminating mutual mistrust. The dialogue should focus on the issues that are of core concern for both communities

And should aim at finding a reasonable, practical and mutually satisfying solution to ending the mutual mistrust.

Attempt to strengthen the civil will within the Muslim community for gradually and adopting Socio-cultural reforms through modern education.

Propose the Government of India for considering the creation of a National Development Commission that will provide comprehensive assistance to the economically less-developed people of India in pursuing their educational studies and professional ventures for economic development. This Commission may have appropriate percentage of its annual budgetary allocation reserved for the minority Communities of India.

Encourage and organise the nation-wide Celebration of a Festival of Harmony on 30th January every year for fostering a strong bond of brotherhood between and amongst various communities in India.

POLITICAL EMPOWERMENT OF WOMEN

The participation of women in politics and in the democratic decision-making process is not very significant at present. In the context of domination of money power and muscle power in electoral politics women find it difficult to contest elections successfully. As a consequence women's presence in the parliament and state legislatures is totally disproportionate to their numerical strength which is almost 50 percent of the total population of India. In the absence of adequate number of women's representatives legislative bodies have tended to sideline women's issues in their legislative business and to be indifferent to introduce laws required to safeguard the rights and dignity of women. As long as women's presence in the legislative bodies is weak it will be difficult to bring in suitable reforms and eradicate all sorts of social evils afflicting women. So it is necessary to create more space for women in the legislative bodies by reserving seats in these bodies in proportion to the numerical strength of women. To this end the bill proposing a reservation of 33 percent of seats in the parliament for quite some time should be passed immediately setting aside for the time being the reservation of seats for SC, BC and OBC women within proposed reserved quote of 33 percent. Further, all political parties talk a lot about improving the status of women and their political and economic empowerment. But the representation of women in their respective organisational structures at national, state and local levels is woefully inadequate. Since political parties are the best training grounds for developing political leadership they must reserve for women 50 percent or at least 33 percent of seats in their various committees and boards without waiting for the parliament to pass the proposed women's reservation bill. Moreover it is also true that women are unwilling to enter politics for various reasons. This obstacle has to be removed by imparting political training to women. Political parties can play a very positive and effective role in this regard by conducting political study, training and motivation camps for women.

The new panchayatraj system has widened the political space for women by reserving 33 percent of seats for women in panchayatraj institutions at various levels. It has opened the doors for several lakhs of women to enter local politics and occupy positions of local leadership. But most of the women elected to these panchayatraj institutions are not aware of their duties and responsibilities as well as their rights and power. Many women representatives of the Dalits are not able to assert themselves and exercise their rights. So they need to be made aware of their rights as well as their responsibilities. NGOs can help in this situation by conducting special training programmes for the benefit of women functionaries and representatives in the Panchayatraj institutions.

Though there are many women's organisations working for the upliftment of women, most of them are working in isolation. So the women's movement is weak and there is need to network the existing women's organisations, and launch a united women's organisation which can exercise a powerful pressure on the state and society to introduce suitable reforms to remove obstacles in the way of women's liberation and empower them to fight for their legitimate rights and dignity as human beings. Moreover, women's organisations tend to adopt a confrontationist attitude to men in their fight for equal status with men. But such a pressure is not effective. So every effort needs to be made to enlist the co-operation and support of men to the struggles of women. There is countless number of men who are equally concerned about the suffering of women. Such men should be identified and roped into their movement. Further, women are not the only oppressed section of the society. There are dalits, tribes, landless peasants, and bonded labour, who are equally oppressed. They are also fighting for their rights and liberation through their own organisation. It will go a long way in furthering the cause of women's liberation, if women's organisation establishes solidarity with them and avail themselves of their organisational strength, leadership and other resources. So women, instead of fighting for their rights in isolation it would go well to join hands with all the exploited and oppressed sections of the society. If all the exploited groups demand their rights as human beings with one voice the walls of power and privilege cannot but come down. The rights of all the exploited and oppressed people-women, dalits, landless peasants, tribals, bonded labours, etc are all human rights. Women can play a major role in uniting all these groups which are deprived of their human rights and fighting against their exploiters and oppressors.

CONCLUSION

Political empowerment adds strengthen to the social empowerment of the socially disabled. These people should have more space in the political process. Apart from the existing reservations for SCs, STs and Backward Classes, conscious efforts should be made to provide the proposed 33% reservation for women in legislature in addition to the existing provision for reservation of 1/3rd seats for women in panchayats and nagar palikas. All the political parties should make it a point to provide adequate number of positions for women in the party organizational structure and reserve 33% seats for women for parliament and state legislative assembly elections. The political parties on the government should also consider for reservation in case of minorities.

CHAPTER-IX
INDIAN DEMOCRACY AND SOCIAL EMPOWERMENT

INTRODUCTION

India is a sovereign, socialist, secular, democratic republic and its Constitution provides to secure to all its citizens justice, liberty, equality and fraternity. The integrity of the nation, its rich cultural heritage and its compositeness, Indian ethos and values, equal respect for all citizens irrespective of caste, creed, colour, gender, region, religion and march towards a bright future, were some of the basic considerations which the Constitution makers had in mind while framing the Constitution of India. Social empowerment plays an important role in a country like India for sustainability of its democracy.

Social empowerment relates to the empowerment of socially disadvantaged groups. These groups still lag behind the rest of the society due to their social and economic backwardness. Their share in the country's total population is quiet substantial. Thus, the empowerment of the socially disadvantaged groups assumes importance. Fulfillment of their constitutional safeguards is vital to sustain the democratic credentials of the country.

CONSTITUTIONAL SAFEGUARDS

Recognising the relative backwardness of the weaker sections of the society, the Constitution of India guarantees equality before the law (Article 14) and enjoins the state to make special provisions for the advancement of any socially and educationally backward classes or for SCs (Article 15(4)). It also empowers the state to make provisions for reservation in appointments or posts in favour of any backward class citizens (Article (16(4)). The Constitution of India also states categorically that untouchabality is abolished and its practice in any form is forbidden (Article 17). Further, it enjoins the state to promote, with special care, the educational and economic interests of the weaker sections of the people and, in particular, of SCs and promises to protect them from social injustice and all forms of exploitation (Article 46). Reservation of seats for SCs in the democratic institutions (Article 330) and in services (Article 335) is another measure of positive discrimination in favour of these groups. It empowers the state to appoint a commission to investigate into the conditions of socially and educationally backward classes (Article 340) and to specify the castes to be deemed as SCs (Article 341).

In the case of Minorities, the Constitution adopts certain safeguards to recognise their rights in conserving their culture and establish and administer educational institutions of their choice under the Articles 29 and 30. While the Article 350(A) advocates instructions in the mother tongue at the primary stage of education to children belonging to Linguistic Minorities, Article 350(B) provides for a special offer to safeguard the interests to the Linguistic Minorities. Besides these specific Articles, there are also a number of Constitutional provisions enabling protection and promotion of the interests of these socially Disadvantaged Groups.

LEGISLATIVE SUPPORT

There exists a plethora of social legislations to safeguard the interests of the persons in distress and to deal with the various social problems/ evils. In pursuance of various constitutional provisions, several child related legislations have been enacted besides adoption of **National Policies for children in 1974** and **National Plan of Action for Children** and another exclusively for **Girl Child in 1992.**

Some of the important legislations are listed below: **The Indian Penal Code, 1860** provides safeguards for protection of children against the cruelties of kidnapping, abduction, prostitution, death etc.; The **Suppression of Immoral Traffic in Women and Girls Act of 1956** was drastically **amended in 1986** and renamed as the **Immoral Traffic (Prevention) Act** for preventing and checking trafficking in women and girls; **The Juvenile Justice Act, 1986** provides for care, protection, treatment, development and rehabilitation of neglected or delinquent juveniles. This **has been replaced by a new legislation Viz. The juvenile Justice (Care and Protection of Children) Act, 2000,** which is more child-friendly and makes a distinction between a juvenile offender and a child in need.

The **Child Marriage Restraint Act, 1929** as **amended in 1976** restrains solemnization of child marriages; **The Hindu Succession Act, 1956** as **amended in 1993** provides equal rights to the daughter in coparcenary property along with the rights of the child in womb and general rules of succession in case of females and males; The

Hindu Adoption and Maintenance Act, 1956 amends and codifies the law relating to adoptions and maintenance among Hindus; **The Registration of Births and Deaths Act, 1969** provides for compulsory and free of charge registration of all births/deaths occurring in the country within 14-21 days of the event. The **Child Labour (Prohibition and Regulation) act 1986** prohibits engagement of children in certain occupations and regulates the conditions of work of children in certain other employments; The **Pre-natal Diagnostic Techniques (Regulation and Prevention on Misuse) 1994** prohibits ante-natal sex determination test to prevent female foeticide.

The State has also enacted the following women specific and women related legislations to protect women against social discrimination, violence and atrocities and also to prevent social evils. **The Hindu Marriage Act of 1955 amended in 1976** provides the right for a girl to repudiate a child marriage before attaining maturity whether the marriage has been consummated or not. The **Factories Act of 1948 (amended upto 1976)** provides for establishment of a crèche where 30 women are employed (including casual and contract labours). The **Medical Termination of Pregnancy Act of 1971** legalises abortion by qualified professional on humanitarian or medical grounds. **Amendments to Criminal Law in 1983** provide for punishment of 7 years ordinary cases of rape and 10 years for custodial rape cases. The **Indecent Representation of Women (Prohibition) act of 1986** and The **Commission of Sati (Prevention) Act, 1987** have also been passed to protect the dignity of women and prevent violence against them as well as their exploitation.

The problem of drug abuse received special attention during Eighties in respect of its control and extending welfare cum rehabilitative services. The **Narcotic Drug and Psychotropic Substances Act of 1985** was amended in 1988 to make the law stringent for effective control over narcotic drugs and psychotropic substances. Subsequently, the **Prevention of Illicit Traffic in Narcotic Drugs and Psychotropic Substances Act (1988)** was passed, which provides for preventive detention of persons trafficking in drugs. The enforcement machinery was also strengthened.

To ensure equal opportunities for persons with disabilities and their full participation in nation building, a comprehensive legislation namely, '**The Persons with Disabilities (Equal Opportunities, Protection of Rights and Full Participation) Act, 1995** was enacted. The Act provides for both preventive and promotional aspects of rehabilitation like education, employment and vocational training, reservation, research and manpower development, creation of barrier-free environment, rehabilitation for persons with disability, unemployment allowance for the disabled, special insurance scheme for the disabled employees and establishment of homes for persons with severe disability etc. The Act has been **amended** In order to improve and further strengthen the scope and the facilities for the benefit of disabled persons. The **Rehabilitation Council if India,** a statutory body was set up under the **RCI Act of 1992.** This body is responsible for regulating professional syllabus and enforcing uniform standards in training professionals and giving them recognition in different areas of disability. The **National Trust for Welfare of Persons with Autism, Cerebral Palsy, Mental Retardation and Multiple Disabilities Act** was passed in December, **1999.** This Trust is a statutory body set up to safeguard the interests and the development of these groups. The Prevention of Beggary Acts which are State Acts also exist in a number of States.

REVIEW

The consultation paper on pace of socio-economic change under the constitution brought out by National Commission to Review the Working of the Constitution (May, 2001) points out that despite manifest, avowed and determined concern of the Constitution for uplift and welfare of the Scheduled Castes, Scheduled Tribes and Backward Classes, the objectives have not been achieved. Whatever has been done in this regard has been done hesitatingly, half-heartedly and as a measure of concession forgetting that this relates to their Constitutional rights and not concession to those classes. Supported by relevant statistics the following observations are made, in the paper, in respect of the Scheduled Castes, Scheduled Tribes and backward classes.

1. The high number of cases registered under the Protection of Civil Rights Act, 1955 and the Scheduled Castes and the Scheduled Tribes (Prevention of Atrocities) Act, 1989 shows that atrocities against Scheduled Castes and the Scheduled Tribes and untouchability continue unabated even today.

2. Representation of Scheduled Castes and Scheduled Tribes in Group 'B' & Group 'A' posts in Central Government itself continues to remain inadequate and Scheduled Tribes are not even adequately represented in Group 'C' and Group 'D' services.

3. The paper notes that the reservation for other backward communities in Central services was provided only in 1990 and became operational from 1993 onwards and sufficient statistical data are not yet available to draw any definite

conclusions to the extent, their reservation has improved in the central services but the adequate representation of backward classes in public services is, still a far cry.

4. Landlessness is increasing amongst the Scheduled Castes and the proportion of the Scheduled Caste agricultural labourers to the Scheduled Caste cultivators is increasing which indicates that the Scheduled Caste cultivators after losing their land holdings are becoming agricultural labourers. The results are not very different for Scheduled Tribes also.

5. Some studies, the paper notes, have pointed out that allocation of funds for the development and welfare of the Scheduled Castes and Scheduled Tribes has shown a steadily declining trend since the late eighties.

6. Allocations for welfare of the Scheduled Castes, the Scheduled Tribes and backward classes do not match their developmental needs and priorities and implementation of schemes makes the matter worse.

EMPOWERMENT OF WOMEN

The consultation paper on Pace of Socio-economic change under the Constitution of the National Commission to Review the Working of the Constitution notes that the full potential of women remains grossly underutilized even after more than 51 years of the working of the Constitution and suggests steps to enhance the representation of women at various levels of policy making and administration and for the process of empowerment of women that began with reservation of one-third seats in Panchayats and municipalities to State Legislatures and Parliament.

Clearance of the pending Bill in the Parliament regarding women's reservation in Parliament and State Assemblies will add in a big measure to the empowerment of women.

The Government adopted a National Policy on empowerment of women in April 2001 and the Country has the mandate to translate the Policy into Action. The objectives of the National Policy for Empowerment of women include: i) creating an environment through positive economic and social policies for full development of women to enable them to realize their full potential; ii) the de-jure and de-facto enjoyment of all human rights and fundamental freedom by women on equal basis with men in all spheres – political, economic, social, cultural and civil; iii) equal access to participation and decision making of women in social, political and economic life of the nation; iv) equal access to women to health care, quality education at all levels, career and vocational guidance, employment, equal remuneration, occupational health hazard safety, social security and public office etc.; v) strengthening legal systems aimed at elimination of all forms of discrimination against women; vi) changing societal attitudes and community practices by active participation and involvement of both men and women; vii) mainstreaming a gender perspective in the development process; viii) elimination of discrimination and all forms of violence against women and the girl child; and ix) building and strengthening partnership with civil society, particularly women's organisations.

SOCIAL EMPOWERMENT

The Tenth Five Year Plan document suggests to create an enabling environment for the welfare and development of the Socially Disadvantaged Groups by removing the still existing inequalities, disparities and other persisting problems besides providing easy and equal access to basic minimum services through:

- Education being the most effective instrument of empowering the Socially Disadvantaged Groups, all-out efforts will be made to improve the educational status of these Groups, especially of Women and the Girl Child.

- Universalisation of primary education by 2007 and at elementary stage by 2010 with a special focus on low literacy pockets, and educationally backward communities viz., SCs, OBCs, Minorities and Women with a special focus on the girl child.

- Improving enrolment/retention rates of these Groups in schools and thus reduce school drop-out rates through special incentives/support services like hostels, financial assistance, scholarships, free books, uniforms etc and thus improve the educational status of these Groups, especially that of their women and girl children.

- Priority to the educational development of the Minorities, especially Muslims, with special focus on women and girl children besides modernising and mainstreaming traditional educational systems/institutions viz. Madarasas by adopting regular educational syllabi.

- Vocational training/education to improve the technical and productive capabilities of these Groups, suiting local needs and market demands.

- Expanding/strengthening national health programmes such as control of Blindness and Tuberculosis, Eradication of Leprosy etc. in the SC/OBC/Minority concentrated areas.

- Supplementing primary health care services through the Pradhan Mantri Gramodaya Yojana (PMGY) so as to fill the critical gaps, both in the infrastructure and services in the SC/OBC/Minority concentrated areas.

- Extending ICDS and RCH to take care of the expectant and nursing mothers and children with a major objective of reducing the existing high Infant/Child maternal Mortality Rates amongst these Groups. Also, help stabilise the population of these Groups.

- 'Reaching the Un-reached' viz. SC/OBC/Minority groups, those living in the most backward and neglected areas, in general and their women and the girl children, in particular through the Universalised/Expanded programmes of ICDS, RCH, Supplementary Nutrition Programme, Mid-Day Meals, PMGY, NNM etc.

- Encouraging the participation of the Socially Disadvantaged Groups in the planning and developmental processes at every level through ensuring their adequate representation in various democratic decision making institutions like Panchayat Raj/Local bodies, State Assemblies/Parliament etc.

To continue the process of Empowering the Socially Disadvantaged Groups viz. SCs, OBCs and Minorities which would help develop their capacities and to become active partners and partakers of country's development and thus raise their status to that of the rest of the society, the Tenth Plan's suggests a social empowerment strategy through the removal of all the still existing inequalities, disparities and other persisting problems besides providing easy access to basic minimum services.

It also suggests social justice strategy through elimination of all types of discrimination against the Socially Disadvantaged Groups with the strength of Constitutional commitments, legislative support, affirmative action, awareness generation, conscientisation of target groups and change in the mind-set of people.

The National Policy for empowerment of women prescribes the following measures for social empowerment of women:

a) Equal access to education for women and girls will be ensured and special measures will be taken to eliminate discrimination, universalize education, eradicate illiteracy, create a gender-sensitive educational system, increase enrolment and retention rates of girls and improve the quality of education to facilitate life-long learning as well as development of occupation/vocation/technical skills by women. Reducing the gender gap in secondary and higher education would be a focus area. Sectoral time targets in existing policies will be achieved, with a special focus on girls and women, particularly those belonging to weaker sections including the Scheduled Castes/Scheduled Tribes/Other Backward Classes/Minorities.

Gender sensitive curricula would be developed at all levels of educational system in order to address sex stereotyping as one of the causes of gender discrimination.

b) A holistic approach to women's health which includes both nutrition and health services will be adopted and special attention will be given to the needs of women at all stages of the life cycle. Measures will be adopted that take into account the reproductive rights of women to enable them to exercise informed choices, their vulnerability to sexual and health problems together with endemic, infectious and communicable diseases such as malaria, TB, and water borne diseases as well as hypertension and cardio-pulmonary diseases. The social, developmental and health consequences of HIV/AIDS and other sexually transmitted diseases will be tackled from a gender perspective.

c) Men and women will have access to safe, effective and affordable methods of family planning of their choice. The child marriages shall be eliminated by 2010 by measures like compulsory registration of marriage, spread of education and programs like BSY.

d) Focused attention would be paid to meeting the nutritional needs of women at all stages of the life cycle, particularly of the adolescent girls and pregnant and lactating mothers.

e) All forms of discrimination against the girl child and violation of her rights shall be eliminated by undertaking strong measures both preventive and punitive within and outside the family. These would relate specifically to strict enforcement of laws against prenatal sex selection and the practices of female foeticide, female infanticide, child marriage, child abuse and child prostitution etc. There will be special emphasis on the needs of the girl child and earmarking of substantial investments in the areas relating to food and nutrition, health and education, and in vocational education.

f)   Special attention will be given to the needs of women in the provision of safe drinking water, sewage disposal, toilet facilities and sanitation within accessible reach of households, especially in rural areas and urban slums.

g)   Special attention will be given for providing adequate and safe housing and accommodation for women including single women, heads of households, working women, students, apprentices and trainees. Women's perspectives will be included in housing policies, planning of housing colonies and provision of shelter both in rural and urban areas.

h)   Measures will be undertaken to provide women in difficult circumstances such as destitute, disabled and old women, women heading households, women affected by natural calamities, those displaced from employment, migrants, deserted women and women who are victims of marital violence and prostitutes etc.

MIND-SETS AND ATTITUDE

The National Commission to Review the Working of the Constitution has rightly pointed out thus:

"There is a need to surmount the colonial hangover of the notion of the 'Ruler' and the 'Ruled', 'governors' and the 'Governed', 'Government' and 'People' – the 'us' and 'they' divide. The interaction between the Administrator and the citizenry needs to be informed by the awareness of and respect for the constitutional rights of the people and that the inter-action is essentially as between a free and self-governing people on the one hand and the agents chosen by them to serve them on the other".

In addition to the above, unless reformation comes in the mind-set of the people in the society in general, the success in social empowerment may not be achieved fully. This change in mind set could be brought about through (a) Media and (b) the Educational System highlighting the need for special treatment of the weaker sections due to historical and other reasons resulting in their oppression and social and economic backwardness.

CHAPTER-X

EFFECTIVENESS OF RESERVATIONS FOR SCHEDULED CASTES AND SCHEDULED TRIBES

INTRODUCTION

As is well known, the Scheduled Castes and the Scheduled Tribes are specified as per provisions in Articles 341 and 342 of the Constitution. The scheduling of castes and tribes enables members of these communities to take advantage of certain benefits. This inter-alia include: -

a)	Political	:	Reservations of seats in Lok Sabha. State Legislatures and also in Local Bodies;
b)	Employment	:	Reservation of vacancies in public services;
c)	Protective	:	Special legislation for protecting economic and social interests of these communities;
d)	Developmental	:	Implementation of special programmes for the educational and socio-economic development of Scheduled Castes and Schedules Tribes including reservation of seats in educational institutions.

I) RESERVATION IN SERVICES

A. PROVISIONS FOR SCHEDULE CASTES

Acknowledging the need for securing a fair degree of representation in public services for the members of the Scheduled Castes, the Government of India issued instructions in July, 1934 that duly qualified candidates from these castes should not be deprived of fair Opportunities of appointments merely because they could not succeed in an open Competition. It was, however, considered not necessary at that time to reserve any percentage of vacancies for them in view of their educational backwardness. When the position was reviewed in 1942 it was revealed that in spite of various measures undertaken to secure increased representation of members of Scheduled Castes in public services the results were not encouraging. The Government of India, therefore, considered that reservation of a definite percentage of vacancies might provide stimulus to candidates of these castes to equip themselves with better qualifications and become eligible for various government posts and services. It was further thought that grant of age concession and reduction in examination fees would also help in securing qualified candidates from among the members of the 201 Scheduled Castes. Considering that sufficient number of candidates from the Scheduled Caste communities would not be forthcoming to avail the number of vacancies to which they were entitled on population ratio which was 12.75 per cent, the Government of India issued orders in August, 1943 reserving 8 1/3% of vacancies for them with a proviso to consider the question of raising the percentage as soon as sufficient number of qualified candidates amongst these communities were found to be available. Initially, the reservation was made applicable only in the case of direct recruitment and not in the case of promotion. The orders applied to Central Services (Class I and II) and subordinate services under the administrative control of Government of India with the exception of a few services and posts for which highly technical or special qualifications were required. The maximum age limit prescribed for appointment to a service or a post was increased by three years in favour of candidates belonging to Scheduled Caste communities and the examination fees prescribed were reduced to 1/4th in their case. In June, 1946, the percentage of vacancies reserved in favour of members of the Scheduled Castes was raised from 8 1/3% to 12 1/2% to correspond to the percentage of population of Scheduled Castes in the country.

Consequent on the attainment of Independence and partition of the country, the communal representation rules were revised. The revised orders provided that in so far as recruitment through open competition was concerned reservation for communities other than Scheduled Castes should be withdrawn and that in the case of the latter the then existing percentage of reservation of 12 1/2% should be continued. In case of recruitment made otherwise than by open competition but made on an all-India basis, it was laid down that 16 2/3% of the vacancies should be reserved for members of the Scheduled Castes.

PROVISIONS FOR SCHEDULED TRIBES

The Government of India also examined the question of providing reservation in Central services for Scheduled Tribes. It was considered that no useful purpose was likely to be served by providing such reservation since members of those tribes were too backward to be available in sufficient numbers for appointment to posts under the Government. Instructions were, however, issued in December, 1947 that the appointing authorities should keep in view the desirability of recruitment of suitable candidates from amongst tribal people in vacancies reserved for other minorities to the extent to which suitable candidates were available particularly in making recruitment from the States of Assam, Bihar, Central Provinces and Berar (now Madhya Pradesh) and Orissa. In July, 1949, orders were issued allowing the tribal people advantage of fees concession as admissible to the members of the Scheduled Castes.

Reservation Policy after coming into effect of the Constitution of India

The Articles -of the Constitution which govern the reservation policy are as under:-

Article 16(4): "Nothing in this Article shall prevent the State from making any provision for the reservation of appointments or posts in favour of any backward class of citizens which in the opinion of the State, is not adequately represented in the services under the State".

Article 46: "The State shall promote with special care the educational and economic interests of the weaker sections of the people, and, in particular, of the Scheduled Castes and the Scheduled Tribes, and shall protect them from social injustice and all forms of exploitation".

Article 335: "The claims of the members of the Scheduled Castes and the Scheduled Tribes shall be taken into consideration, consistently with the maintenance of efficiency of administration in the making of appointments to services and posts in connection with the affairs of the Union or of a State".

Articles 16(4) and 46:Article 46 charges the State with promoting the economic interests of the weaker sections and, in particular, of the

Scheduled Castes and Tribes. But the provisions of Article 46 are not enforceable by the Courts, and had there been no provision like Clause (4) of Article 16, any reservation of posts for the backward classes would have been void on account of inconsistency with Clause (1) of Article 16. But the protection of backward classes may require appointment of members of such classes in the State services. Hence, such provision has been made by including Clause (4) in Article 16.

Articles 16 (4) and 335:

The provisions of Article 335 should be taken into consideration along with Article 16 (4). While Article 335 relates specifically to Scheduled Castes and Tribes, Clause (4) of Article 16 refers to 'Backward Classes' generally. While Article 16 (4) authorises the State to make 'reservation' of posts, Article 335 authorises the State to appoint persons belonging to these Castes and Tribes to any post without such reservation, having regard only to the 'efficiency of administration'.

Since Scheduled Castes and Tribes, prima facie, come within the expression 'backward classes', it may seem that there is a conflict between the two provisions in Articles 16 (4) and 335 but there need not necessarily be any conflict. Article 16 (4) does not come into operation until and unless there is a 'reservation' made by the State by legislation or by some executive declaration. But even without such 'reservation' the State is enjoined, by Article 335 to consider the special claims of members of Scheduled Castes and Tribes in the making of particular appointments 'consistently with the maintenance of efficiency of administration'. It is to be noted, on the other hand, that the provision in Clause (4) of Article 16 is not mandatory but merely enabling.

Relevance of Reservation Policy

The ultimate objective for providing reservation for Scheduled Castes and Scheduled Tribes in Civil posts and services of the Government is not merely to give employment to some persons but to uplift them socially and educationally and also to enable them to participate in national endeavors as equal partners. In this connection, it is appropriate to quote what the Study Team on Tribal Development Programmes (Chairman - Shilu Ao, 1969) observed:

"As a measure calculated to promote the material welfare and improve the socioeconomic condition of the tribals the Study Team attaches the greatest importance to the implementation, in letter as well as in spirit, of the provisions of the Constitution bearing on the reservation of posts in Government service for the members of the Scheduled Tribes. It is true that agriculture is the mainstay of the tribals in most parts of the country but as suitable land available for assignment is scarce and cannot meet even a small fraction of the demand, the scope for ameliorating the lot of tribals through the promotion of agriculture is limited. The benefits of the concession regarding the reservation of posts are many and varied. A tribal who enters Government service, particularly in the middle or higher echelons, is not only benefited economically but acquire a social standing and a certain measure of sophistication which are almost certain to impel him to give to his children an education and an upbringing such as will ensure for them a status not inferior to the status which he himself has attained. To the individual, therefore, entry into Government service is at once a privilege and an opportunity; to his children it means a better start and a new and fuller life; and to the community to which he belongs a source of inspiration, shaking them out of their lethargy and encouraging them to emulate the success of one of their members".

One cannot also resist quoting in this context what Toynbee observed (The Study of History of Toynbee quoted from the Report of the First Backward Classes Commission, 1955) "that out of twenty civilizations that went down the hill in the course of history, fifteen failed to adjust the competing claims of different sections of the population It has, therefore, been recognized more as a measure of State-craft than as a philosophic doctrine that the internal stability of a country cannot be maintained unless all the various strata of the population are given a fair share in the administration of the country".

In September, 1950, the Government of India, in cancellation of all previous orders on the subject of reservation, issued fresh instructions. Under these orders, the following main provisions were made for the members of the Scheduled Castes and the Scheduled Tribes in matters of recruitment.

A) Scheduled Castes: -

    i. Reservation of 12 1/2% of vacancies filled by direct recruitment in the case of recruitment to posts and services made on an all-India basis by open competition, that is, through the Union Public Service Commission or by means of open competitive tests held by any other authority.

    ii. Reservation of 16 2/3% of vacancies filled by direct recruitment in the case of recruitment to posts and services made on an all-India basis, otherwise than by open competition.

B) Scheduled Tribes:-

Reservation of 5% of vacancies filled by direct recruitment both in recruitment by open competition and in recruitment made otherwise than by open competition.

C) Both for Scheduled Castes and Scheduled Tribes:-

i. In the case of recruitment made otherwise than through the Union Public Service Commission, and for which only those residing in the area or locality in which office where vacancies have occurred, is situated, are likely to apply, the percentage of reservation is fixed by taking into account the population of those Castes and Tribes in that area.

ii. The maximum age limit prescribed for appointment to a service or post is increased by three years.

iii. Fee prescribed for admission to any examination or selection in matters of recruitment is reduced to one-fourth.

These orders were applicable to all services under the control of the Government of India including posts and services in Part C States. It was also decided that if in any year, the quota of reserved vacancies is not fully utilized, the balance was to be carried forward to the next year but not to subsequent years.

In the early stages of implementation of the reservation policy, the progress apparently was slow. In the Third Report, for the year 1953, of the Commissioner for Scheduled Castes and Scheduled Tribes, number of SC/ST employees in the Central Government services has been given, which is reproduced below:-

Statement showing the total number of Scheduled Castes and Scheduled Tribes employed in the Ministries of the Government of India and its attached and subordinate offices (excluding Ministries of Railways. Communication, Finance, Information and Broadcasting) and in the organisations under its control as on 1.12.1952.

In regard to the reservation policy of the State Governments, the Commissioner for Scheduled Castes and Scheduled Tribes in his report for the year ending 1951 stated:- "The only comments that I want to make on.the recruitment policy of the State Governments is that the State Governments which have not made separate reservation in services for Scheduled Castes and Scheduled Tribes, should revise their existing orders on the subject with a view to giving separate reservation to these castes and tribes. There appears to be an impression that under the provisions of the Constitution such a reservation cannot be made. I do not agree with the view. Article 335 read with Article 16 (4) of the Constitution leaves no room for any doubt for fixing separate reservation for Scheduled Castes and Scheduled Tribes". He further observed that "from whatever information I have received so far, it can be safely concluded that the position of Scheduled Castes and Scheduled Tribes in matters of recruitment is not what it should be".

Nature of Post	Permanent Posts			Temporary Posts		
	Actual Strength	SCs.	STs.	Actual Strength	SCs.	STs.
1	2	3	4	5	6	7
Class I	752	10	2	2688	16	4
Class II (Gazetted)	642	7	3	3249	44	21

(Contd.)

Nature of Post	Permanent Posts			Temporary Posts		
	Actual Strength	SCs.	STs.	Actual Strength	SCs.	STs.
Class III	10372	536	71	95079	3071	547
Class IV	8870	1251	119	162161	32257	1499
Unclassified	2390	464	24	3746	667	217
Total	24149	2312	226	271389	36083	2291

After the issue of orders in September, 1950, the Government of India issued further instructions and orders inter-alia revising the percentage of reservation; rule regarding 'carry forward', extension of reservation to promotion posts etc., from time to time. The provisions after the passage of over a few decades of launching the reservation policy, concessions available to Scheduled Caste and Scheduled Tribe applicants are as follows:-

CHAPTER-XI

THE COMMON MAN IN THE INDIAN DEMOCRACY

Common Man

Who is a Common Man? There are many definitions as follows:

- The undistinguished commoner lacking class or rank distinction or special attributes.

- **common man** - a person who holds no title

  common person, commoner

  individual, mortal, person, somebody, someone, soul -

- a human being; "there was too much for one person to do"

  bourgeois, burgher - a member of the middle class

  nobody, nonentity, cypher, cipher - a person of no influence

  everyman - the ordinary person

  Joe Bloggs, Joe Blow, John Doe, man in the street -

- a hypothetical average man

layman, layperson, secular -

- someone who is not a clergyman or a professional person

pleb, plebeian - one of the common people

- **prole, proletarian, worker** - a member of the working class (not necessarily employed); "workers of the world-- unite!"

rustic - an unsophisticated country person (Based on WordNet 3.0, Farlex clipart collection. © 2003-2012 Princeton University, Farlex Inc.)

From the above definitions we may safely assume a Common Man as" An Ordinary Person". That being the case, the Common Man encompasses the whole population of the Country including the General Public, The Scheduled Castes, The Scheduled Tribes, Minorities, and Other Backward Classes.

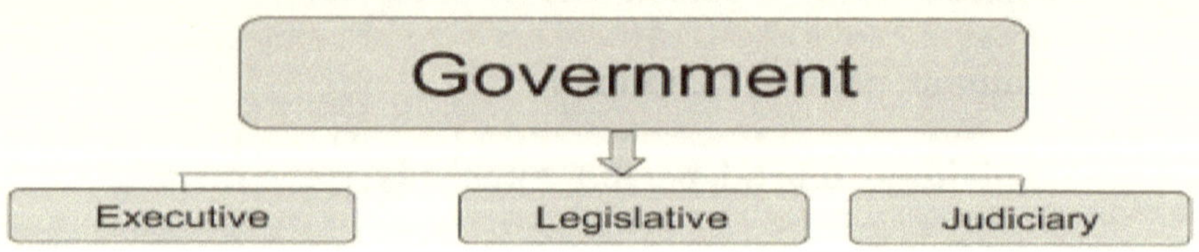

As is well known, Democracy is defined as the government of the people, by the people and for the people. Democracy is considered the most acceptable form of government in which every individual participates consciously and in which the people remain the sovereign power determining their destiny. The democratic Government consists of Three Wings of Governance:

THE COMMON MAN AND THE GOVERNMENT

A. Government's welfare, development and security Programmes

Since 1947 many Governments under various political parties have ruled the Country. They formulated and implemented many welfare, development and peace and security programmes for the ordinary persons.

The Father of the Nation, Mohandas Karamchand Gandhi, was the leader of the Indian independence movement against British colonial rule. Employing nonviolent civil disobedience, Gandhi led India to independence and inspired movements for civil rights and freedom across the world. Gandhi's birthday, October 2, is commemorated in India as Gandhi Jayanti, a national holiday, and worldwide as the International Day of Nonviolence. Pundit Jawaharlal Nehru, the First Prime Minister of India, became the Architect of Modern India. Babasaheb Dr Bhimrao Ramji Ambedkar was a scholar, a social reformer and a leader who dedicated his life to eradicating social inequality in India. He established an India of equals, a country that provided more significant opportunities for historically disadvantaged people. The struggle was a part of Babasaheb's life as he had to work hard for everything he achieved. While he is remembered for his relentless crusade for a new social order, the Indian nation shall always remain indebted to him for giving India a Constitution that defines its core values as a nation. He was the man who made us a nation of equals. The Iron Man Of India, Vallabhbhai Jhaverbhai Patel, was a senior leader of the Indian National Congress who played a leading role in the Country's struggle for independence and guided its integration a united, independent nation. Patel took charge of the integration of the princely states into India. This achievement formed the cornerstone of Patel's popularity in the post-independence era. Even today, he is remembered as the man who united India. The Iron Lady of India, Smt. Indira Gandhi took a bold step of nationalising the Banks for the benefit of the weaker sections of the Society when she was the Prime Minister of India. Shri Rajiv Gandhi being the Youngest Prime Minister, boosted the application of Science and Technology. Shri P.V. Narasimha Rao, as Prime minister, saved the Country from Economic collapse. He also introduced the 'Panchayat Raj' System in the Country. Shri Vishwanath Pratap Singh, as Prime Minister, took the bold step of introducing Reservation for Backward Classes. Likewise, the other Governments also presented programmes for the Common Man. The List of Various Prime Ministers since Independence is provided in Annexure-III.

The Common Man include the S.Cs and S.Ts.The S.Ts are the most backward among the weaker sections. A Note on S.Cs and S.Ts(Annexure-IV),Scheduled Castes(Annexure-V) and Scheduled Tribes(Annexure-VI) are attached.

As an illustration and testimony, the copy of the Profile of the Author as the Rise of a Commonman from a Scheduled Tribe of first generation is attached as Annexure-VII. A book has also been published on his Autobiography titled 'THE RISE OF A TRIBAL' which relates to his Life History presented as 'AN AUTOBIOGRAPHY' of a Tribal. The Autobiography is the Life Journey of a poor, first generation learner, a highly educated and a scheduled tribe of Andhra Pradesh, India and traces his childhood spent in utter poverty subjected to social discrimination and humiliation. Undaunted by these hardships and with sheer determination he rose to higher levels of education, official positions and in his self efforts, using the provisions of the Indian

Freedom, Democracy and its Constitution and parental support as a stepping ladder. Dr. Baba Saheb Ambedkar as a source of inspiration, and taking the poverty as a challenge, he could pursue higher education in England and obtained his PhD in Structural Engineering from the University of Liverpool after hard working while leaving his family of mother, wife and four small children in India for three years. This hard earned degree worked as a spring board to be selected as Deputy Secretary (latter on to become the Joint Secretary and the Additional Secretary) in University Grants Commission(UGC),New Delhi and later to be invited by late Shri N.T.Rama Rao, the then Chief Minister Of Andhra Pradesh) to become the Vice-Chancellor of the then Jawaharlal Nehru Technological University,Hyderabad.Even before completing the Vice-Chancellor's term, he was invited by the Prime Ministers of India to become a Member of the erstwhile Planning Commission, Government of India twice (by Shri Chandrasekhar and Shri P.V.Narasimha Rao) and later as a Member of the National Advisory Council(NAC) under Chairmanship of Mrs. Sonia Gandhi. He became the Global Chairman of the prestigious World Intellectual Forum (WIF), Hyderabad which has Global Regional Centers in France(Paris),Arizona(USA),Melbourne (Australia), New York (USA) and Costa Rica being developed. The Author in his simple style narrated his life experiences.

Dr. Swaminadhan proposed for the formation of a New World Government in place of the United Nations (UNO).

Constitutional Reservations should continue until at least the majority of these communities develop on par with the other sections of society.

The Leadership of Dr. B. R. Ambedkar brought solace and constitutional safeguards for the development and welfare of S.Cs and S.Ts. Now what is needed is Individual leadership supported by the beneficiaries, to oversee the sincere implementation of all the constitutional provisions meant for these hapless S.Cs and S.Ts. Eventhough there are already Specific Ministries and Commissions available, but they are official Instruments and therefore, adequate objectivity may be lacking and above all normally they act only when something brought to their notice and suomotto action is limited. The Autobiography of the Author is to serve only as a source of inspiration and instill confidence in S.Cs and S.Ts and feel that they are second to none as far as merit is considered. With utmost humility, it may be stated that, the author providing an innovative approach for the formation of a Federal, Democratic, and a Presidential Form of World Government with its Structure and World Constitution and publishing a book in this regard, is a testimony to this. As we are proud of Dr Baba Saheb Ambedkar for providing the Constitution of India, one should be equally proud that the Auto biographer has provided a World Constitution for a New World Federal Government.

B. PARTICIPATION OF COMMON MAN IN LEGISLATURE

Participation in the Election Process- to elect or get elected.

India is a country divided into states and union territories, with a parliamentary system governed under the Constitution of India, which defines the power distribution among the federal government and the states.

The Indian Legislature comprises the Lok Sabha (House of the People) and the Rajya Sabha (Council of States) forming both the Parliament's Houses. Similarly, at the States level, it has Legislative Assemblies and Legislative Councils. At local levels, there are Panchayat and Municipal Elections.

Thus Elections in India include elections for:

- Members of the Parliament in Lok Sabha and Rajya Sabha,

- Members of State Legislative Assemblies (and also Assembly elections to some of the Union Territories like Delhi),

- Members of State Legislative Councils,

- Members in village panchayats or city corporation councils.

- By-election is held when a person of a particular constituent dies, resigns, or is disqualified.

Common Man

1. As a registered Voter, he can vote for his chosen candidate through a Ballot Box or an EVM system.

2. He is also free to stand for Elections and contest as a political party candidate or as an Independent.

Nowadays, the Election Process involves heavy expenditure. So with some self-financial backup, one can manage as a candidate sponsored by a political party.

But can a Common Man or an honest citizen with no financial background fight elections as an Independent Candidate?

Should then they forego their Constitutional right to contest? What is the Constitutional remedy, then? **The Government should fund the election of a genuine Common man and the honest citizen who want to contest elections.**

Electoral Reforms and Constitutional Amendment may be needed to remedy the situation.

C. JUDICIAL REMEDY

India has a single integrated judicial system that is independent. The judiciary in India has a pyramid**al** structure with the Supreme Court (SC) at the top. High Courts are below the SC, and below them are the district and subordinate courts. The lower courts function under the direct superintendence of the higher courts.

Every citizen has equal access to judicial redressal. The individual can argue his case independently or has to engage a lawyer to present his case. It is fine as far as the litigant can hire a lawyer when he can afford it. But what is the plight of a common poor man who can not afford to engage a lawyer or argue his case himself?The government is providing 'Legal Aid' to the poor. But how many of the poor are aware of it and utilising it? And can we rely on the sincerity of the legal Aid People because the client is not paying anything and depends on what is provided by the Government?

Instead, a "Legal Aid Fund" could be established, and when the Common Man engages a Lawyer, he could be paid from this Fund.

D. Government Service to the Poor

a) It is good that some State Governments are providing all services through a single-window **means** named "Seva Centres". Payment of Old-age Pensions, compensations etc., are credited to their Bank Accounts.

But when the Common Man has to do rounds around Government Offices for land, house etc., problems, they are subjected to negligence, harassment, corruption and abnormal delays. Influential and well-to-do people can get things done.

To ease such problems, each Government Department should identify a 'Coordinating Officer' to help the Common Man get his problem solved.

b) One state **Government** in Andhra Pradesh introduced the concept of "Prajala vaddaku Palana"**(Government going to the people)** and allotted a certain period of the year for this purpose. **This could also ease the ordinary person's problem.**

ANNEXURES

ANNEXURE-I

INDIA AT A GLANC

Background

India is one of the oldest civilizations globally, with a kaleidoscopic variety and rich cultural heritage. It has achieved all-round socio-economic progress since its Independence. India has become self-sufficient in agricultural production and is now one of the top industrialized countries in the world and one of the few nations to have gone into outer space to conquer nature for the people's benefit. It covers an area of 32,87,263 sq. km, extending from the snow-covered Himalayan heights to the south's tropical rain forests. As the 7th largest country globally, India stands apart from the rest of Asia, marked off as it is by mountains and the sea, which give the country a distinct geographical entity. Bounded by the Great Himalayas in the north, it stretches southwards and, at the Tropic of Cancer, tapers off into the Indian Ocean between the Bay of Bengal on the east and the Arabian Sea the west.

Lying entirely in the northern hemisphere, the mainland extends between latitudes 8° 4' and 37° 6' north, longitudes 68° 7' and 97° 25' east and measures about 3,214 km from north to south between the extreme latitudes and about 2,933 km from east to west between the extreme longitudes. It has a land frontier of about 15,200 km. The mainland's coastline, Lakshadweep Islands and Andaman & Nicobar Islands, are 7,516.6 km.

Geography

Geographical information about India

Particulars	Description
Location	The Indian peninsula is separated from mainland Asia by the Himalayas. The Country is surrounded by the Bay of Bengal in the east, the Arabian Sea in the west, and the Indian Ocean to the south.
Geographic Coordinates	Lying entirely in the Northern Hemisphere, the Country extends between 8° 4' and 37° 6' latitudes north of the Equator, and 68° 7' and 97° 25' longitudes east of it.
Indian Standard Time	GMT + 05:30
Area	3.3 Million sq. km
Telephone Country Code	+91
Border Countries	Afghanistan and Pakistan to the north-west; China, Bhutan and Nepal to the north; Myanmar to the east; and Bangladesh to the east of West Bengal. Sri Lanka is separated from India by a narrow sea channel formed by Palk Strait and the Gulf of Mannar.

Coastline	7,516.6 km encompassing the mainland, Lakshadweep Islands, and the Andaman & Nicobar Islands.
Climate	The climate of India can broadly be classified as a tropical monsoon one. But, despite much of India's northern part lying beyond the tropical zone, the entire country has a tropical climate marked by relatively high temperatures and dry winters. There are four seasons: winter (December-February) summer (March-June) south-west monsoon season (June-September) post monsoon season (October-November)
Terrain	The mainland comprises four regions: the great mountain zone, plains of the Ganga and the Indus, the desert region, and the southern peninsula.
Natural Resources	Coal, iron ore, manganese ore, mica, bauxite, petroleum, titanium ore, chromite, natural gas, magnesite, limestone, arable land, dolomite, barytes, kaolin, gypsum, apatite, phosphorite, steatite, fluorite, etc.
Natural Hazards	Monsoon floods, flash floods, earthquakes, droughts, and landslides.
Environment - Current Issues	Air pollution control, energy conservation, solid waste management, oil and gas conservation, forest conservation, etc.

(Contd.)

Particulars	Description
Environment - International Agreements	Rio Declaration on environment and development, Cartagena Protocol on biosafety, Kyoto Protocol to the United Nations Framework Convention on climatic change, World Trade Agreement, Helsinki Protocol to LRTAP on the reduction of sulphur emissions of nitrogen oxides or their transboundary fluxes (Nox Protocol), and Geneva Protocol to LRTAP concerning the control of emissions of volatile organic compounds or their transboundary fluxes (VOCs Protocol).
Geography - Note	India occupies a major portion of the south Asian subcontinent.

People

Information about Indian Citizens

Particulars	Description
Population	India's population, as on 1 March 2011 stood at 1,210,193,422 (623.7 million males and 586.4 million females)
Population Growth Rate	The average annual exponential growth rate stands at 1.64 per cent during 2001-2011
Birth Rate	The Crude Birth rate was 18.3 in 2009

Death Rate	The Crude Death rate was 7.3 in 2009
Life Expectancy Rate	65.8 years (Males); 68.1 years (Females) in the period 2006-2011
Sex Ratio	940 according to the 2011 census
Nationality	Indian
Ethnic Groups	All the five major racial types - Australoid, Mongoloid, Europoid, Caucasian, and Negroid find representation among the people of India.
Religions	According to the 2001 census, out of the total population of 1,028 million in the Country, Hindus constituted the majority with 80.5%, Muslims came second at 13.4%, followed by Christians, Sikhs, Buddhists, Jains, and others.
Languages	There are 22 different languages that have been recognised by the Constitution of India, of which Hindi is an Official Language. Article 343(3) empowered Parliament to provide by law for continued use of English for official purposes.
Literacy	According to the provisional results of the 2011 census, the literacy rate in the Country stands at 74.04 per cent, 82.14% for males and 65.46% for females.

Government

Information about Indian Government

Particulars	Description
Country Name	Republic of India; Bharat Ganrajya
Government Type	Sovereign Socialist Democratic Republic with a Parliamentary system of Government.
Capital	New Delhi
Administrative Divisions	28 States and 8 Union Territories.
Independence	15th August 1947 (From the British Colonial Rule)
Constitution	The Constitution of India came into force on 26th January 1950.
Legal System	The Constitution of India is the fountain source of the legal system in the Country.
Executive Branch	The President of India is the Head of the State, while the Prime Minister is the Head of the Government, and runs office with the support of the Council of Ministers who form the Cabinet Ministry.
Legislative Branch	The Indian Legislature comprises of the Lok Sabha (House of the People) and the Rajya Sabha (Council of States) forming both the Houses of the Parliament.

Judicial Branch	The Supreme Court of India is the apex body of the Indian legal system, followed by other High Courts and subordinate Courts.
Flag Description	The National Flag is a horizontal tricolour of deep saffron (kesaria) at the top, white in the middle, and dark green at the bottom in equal proportion. At the centre of the white band is a navy blue wheel, which is a representation of the Ashoka Chakra at Sarnath.
National Days	26th January (Republic Day) 15th August (Independence Day) 2nd October (Gandhi Jayanti; Mahatma Gandhi's Birthday)

Source: *Ministry of Environment, NITI Aayog, Ministry of Health, Press Information Bureau, Census of India, Ministry of External Affairs, Union Budget, Reserve Bank of India.*

ANNEXURE-II

Constitution of India

The Constitution of India is the supreme law of India. The document lays down the framework demarcating fundamental political code, structure, procedures, powers, and duties of government institutions and sets out fundamental rights, directive principles, and the duties of citizens. It is the longest written constitution of any country on earth. B. R. Ambedkar, chairman of the drafting committee, is widely considered to be its chief architect.

Constitution of India	
Jurisdiction	India
Ratified	26 November 1949; 72 years ago
Date effective	26 January 1950; 71 years ago
System	Federal Parliamentary Constitutional Republic
Branches	Three (Executive, Legislature and Judiciary)
Chambers	Two (Rajya Sabha and Lok Sabha)
Executive	Prime minister-led cabinet responsible to the lower house of the parliament
Judiciary	Supreme court, high courts and district courts
Federalism	Federal

(Contd.)

Constitution of India	
Electoral college	Yes, for presidential and vice-presidential elections
Entrenchments	2
Amendments	104
Last amended	25 January 2020 (104th)
Citation	*Constitution of India (PDF), 9 September 2020, archived from the original (PDF) on 29 September 2020*
Location	Parliament House, New Delhi, India
Author(s)	B. R. Ambedkar Chairman of the Drafting Committee Benegal Narsing Rau Constitutional Advisor to the Constituent Assembly Surendra Nath Mukherjee Chief Draftsman of the Constituent Assembly. and other members of Constituent Assembly
Signatories	284 members of the Constituent Assembly
Supersedes	Government of India Act 1935 Indian Independence Act 1947

It imparts constitutional supremacy (not parliamentary supremacy, since it was created by a constituent assembly rather than Parliament) and was adopted by its people with a declaration in its preamble. Parliament cannot override the constitution.

It was adopted by the Constituent Assembly of India on 26 November 1949 and became effective on 26 January 1950. The constitution replaced the Government of India Act 1935 as the country's fundamental governing document, and the Dominion of India became the Republic of India. To ensure constitutional autochthony, its framers repealed prior acts of the British parliament in Article 395. India celebrates its constitution on 26 January as Republic Day.

The constitution declares India a sovereign, socialist, secular, democratic republic, assuring its citizens justice, equality and liberty, and endeavours to promote fraternity. The original 1950 constitution is preserved in a helium-filled case at the Parliament House in New Delhi. The words "secular" and "socialist" were added to the preamble in 1976 during the Emergency.

Babasaheb Ambedkar, chairman of the drafting committee, presenting the final draft of the Indian constitution to Constituent Assembly president Rajendra Prasad on 25 November 1949

In 1928, the All Parties Conference convened a committee in Lucknow to prepare the Constitution of India, which was known as the Nehru Report.

Most of the colonial India was under British rule from 1857 to 1947. From 1947 to 1950, the same legislation continued to be implemented as India was a dominion of Britain for these three years, as each princely state was convinced by Sardar Patel and V.P.Menon to sign the articles of integration with India, and the British government continued to be responsible for the external security of the country.Thus, the constitution of India repealed the Indian Independence Act 1947 and Government of India Act 1935 when it became effective on 26 January 1950. India ceased to be a dominion of the British Crown and became a sovereign democratic republic with the constitution. Articles 5, 6, 7, 8, 9, 60, 324, 366, 367, 379, 380, 388, 391, 392, 393, and 394 of the constitution came into force on 26 November 1949, and the remaining articles became effective on 26 January 1950.

Previous legislation

The constitution was drawn from a number of sources. Mindful of India's needs and conditions, its framers borrowed features of previous legislation such as the Government of India Act 1858, the Indian Councils Acts of 1861, 1892 and 1909, the Government of India Acts 1919 and 1935, and the Indian Independence Act 1947. The latter, which led to the creation of India and Pakistan, divided the former Constituent Assembly in two. Each new assembly had sovereign power to draft and enact a new constitution for the separate states.

Constituent Assembly

1950 Constituent Assembly meeting
Jawaharlal Nehru signing the constitution

The assembly's final session convened on 24 January 1950. Each member signed two copies of the constitution, one in Hindi and the other in English. The original constitution is hand-written, with each page decorated by artists from Shantiniketan including Beohar

Rammanohar Sinha and Nandalal Bose. Its calligrapher was Prem Behari Narain Raizada. The constitution was published in Dehradun and photolithographed by the Survey of India. Production of the original constitution took nearly five years. Two days later, on 26 January 1950, it became the law of India. The estimated cost of the Constituent Assembly was ₹6.3 crore (million). The constitution has had more than 100 amendments since it was enacted.

Structure

The Indian constitution is the world's longest for a sovereign nation. At its enactment, it had 395 articles in 22 parts and 8 schedules. At about 145,000 words, it is the second-longest active constitution—after the Constitution of Alabama—in the world.

The constitution has a preamble and 470 articles, which are grouped into 25 parts. With 12 schedules[d] and five appendices, it has been amended 104 times; the latest amendment became effective on 14 January 2019.

The constitution's articles are grouped into the following parts:

- *Preamble*, with the words "socialist", "secular" and 'integrity' added in 1976 by the 42nd amendment

- *Part I* – States and union territories

- *Part II* – Citizenship

- *Part III* – Fundamental Rights

- *Part IV[* – Directive Principles of State Policy

- *Part IVA* – Fundamental Duties

- *Part V* – The union

- *Part V* – The states

- *Part VII* – States in the B part of the first schedule *(repealed)*

- *Part VIII* – Union territories

- *Part IX* – Panchayats

- *Part IXA]* – Municipalities

- *Part IXB* – Co-operative societie[

- *Part X* – Scheduled and tribal areas

- *Part XI* – Relations between the union and the states*Part XII* – Finance, property, contracts and suits

- *Part XIII* – Trade and commerce within India

- *Part XIV* – Services under the union and states

- *Part XIVA* – Tribunals

- *Part XV* – Elections

- *Part XVI* – Special provisions relating to certain classes

- *Part XVII* – Languages

- *Part XVIII* – Emergency provisions

- *Part XIX* – Miscellaneous

- *Part XX* – Amending the constitution

- *Part XXI* – Temporary, transitional and special provisions

Appendices

- *Appendix I* – The Constitution (Application to Jammu and Kashmir) Order, 1954

- *Appendix II* – Re-statement, referring to the constitution's present text, of exceptions and modifications applicable to the state of Jammu and Kashmir

- *Appendix III* – Extracts from the Constitution (Forty-fourth Amendment) Act, 1978

- *Appendix IV* – The Constitution (Eighty-sixth Amendment) Act, 2002

- *Appendix V* – The Constitution (Eighty-eighth Amendment) Act, 2003

Governmental sources of power

The executive, legislative, and judicial branches of government receive their power from the constitution and are bound by it. With the aid of its constitution, India is governed by a parliamentary system of government with the executive directly accountable to the legislature.

- Under Articles 52 and 53: the president of India is head of the executive branch

- Under Article 60: the duty of preserving, protecting, and defending the constitution and the law.

- Under Article 74: the prime minister is the head of the Council of Ministers, which aids and advises the president in the performance of their constitutional duties.

- Under Article 75(3): the Council of Ministers is answerable to the lower house.

The constitution is considered federal in nature, and unitary in spirit. It has features of a federation, including a codified, supreme constitution; a three-tier governmental structure (central, state and local); division of powers; bicameralism; and an independent judiciary. It also possesses unitary features such as a single constitution, single citizenship, an integrated judiciary, a flexible constitution, a strong central government, appointment of state governors by the central government, All India Services (the IAS, IFS and IPS), and emergency provisions. This unique combination makes it quasi-federal in form

Each state and union territory has its own government. Analogous to the president and prime minister, each has a governor or (in union territories) a lieutenant governor and a chief minister. Article 356 permits the president to dismiss a state government and assume direct authority if a situation arises in which state government cannot be conducted in accordance with constitution. This power, known as president's rule, was abused as state governments came to be dismissed on flimsy grounds for political reasons. After the *S. R. Bommai v. Union of India* decision, such a course of action is more difficult since the courts have asserted their right of review.

The 73rd and 74th Amendment Acts introduced the system of panchayati raj in rural areas and Nagar Palikas in urban areas. Article 370 gave special status to the state of Jammu and Kashmir.

The Legislature and amendments

Article 368 dictates the procedure for constitutional amendments. Amendments are additions, variations or repeal of any part of the constitution by Parliament. An amendment bill must be passed by each house of Parliament by a two-thirds majority of its total membership when at least two-thirds are present and vote. Certain amendments pertaining to the constitution's federal nature must also be ratified by a majority of state legislatures.

Unlike ordinary bills in accordance with Article 245 (except for money bills), there is no provision for a joint session of the Lok Sabha and Rajya Sabha to pass a constitutional amendment. During a parliamentary recess, the president cannot promulgate ordinances under his legislative powers under Article 123, Chapter III. Deemed amendments to the constitution which can be passed under the legislative powers of parliament were invalidated by Article 368(1) in the 24th Amendment.

By July 2018, 124 amendment bills had been presented in Parliament; of these, 103 became Amendment Acts. Despite the supermajority requirement for amendments to pass, the Indian constitution is the world's most frequently-amended national governing document. The constitution is so specific in spelling out government powers that many amendments address issues dealt with by statute in other democracies.

In 2000, the Justice Manepalli Narayana Rao Venkatachaliah Commission was formed to examine a constitutional update. The government of India establishes term-based law commissions to recommend legal reforms, facilitating the rule of law.

Limitations

In *Kesavananda Bharati v. State of Kerala*, the Supreme Court ruled that an amendment cannot destroy what it seeks to modify; it cannot tinker with the constitution's basic structure or framework, which are immutable. Such an amendment will be declared invalid, although no part of the constitution is protected from amendment; the basic structure doctrine does not protect any one provision of the constitution. According to the doctrine, the constitution's basic features (when "read as a whole") cannot be abridged or abolished. These "basic features" have not been fully defined,] and whether a particular provision of the constitution is a "basic feature" is decided by the courts

The *Kesavananda Bharati v. State of Kerala* decision laid down the constitution's basic structure

1. Supremacy of the constitution

2. Republican, democratic form of government

3. Its secular nature

4. Separation of powers

5. Its federal character

This implies that Parliament can only amend the constitution to the limit of its basic structure. The Supreme Court or a high court may declare the amendment null and void if this is violated, after a judicial review. This is typical of parliamentary governments, where the judiciary checks parliamentary power.

In its 1967 *Golak Nath v. State of Punjab* decision, the Supreme Court ruled that the state of Punjab could not restrict any fundamental rights protected by the basic structure doctrine. The extent of land ownership and practice of a profession, in this case, were considered fundamental rights. The ruling was overturned with the ratification of the 24th Amendment in 1971.

The Judiciary

The judiciary is the final arbiter of the constitution. Its duty (mandated by the constitution) is to act as a watchdog, preventing any legislative or executive act from overstepping constitutional bounds.] The judiciary protects the fundamental rights of the people (enshrined in the constitution) from infringement by any state body, and balances the conflicting exercise of power between the central government and a state (or states).

The courts are expected to remain unaffected by pressure exerted by other branches of the state, citizens or interest groups. An independent judiciary has been held as a basic feature of the constitution, which cannot be changed by the legislature or the executive.

Judicial review

Judicial review was adopted by the constitution of India from judicial review in the United States. In the Indian constitution, judicial review is dealt with in Article 13. The constitution is the supreme power of the nation, and governs all laws. According to **Article 13**:

1. All pre-constitutional laws, if they conflict wholly or in part with the constitution, shall have all conflicting provisions deemed ineffective until an amendment to the constitution ends the conflict; the law will again come into force if it is compatible with the constitution as amended (the Doctrine of Eclipse).

2. Laws made after the adoption of the constitution must be compatible with it, or they will be deemed void *ab initio*.

3. In such situations, the Supreme Court (or a high court) determines if a law is in conformity with the constitution. If such an interpretation is not possible because of inconsistency (and where separation is possible), the provision which is inconsistent with the constitution is considered void. In addition to Article 13, Articles 32, 226 and 227 provide the constitutional basis for judicial review.

Due to the adoption of the Thirty-eighth Amendment, the Supreme Court was not allowed to preside over any laws adopted during a state of emergency which infringe fundamental rights under article 32 (the right to constitutional remedies). The Forty-second Amendment widened Article 31C and added Articles 368(4) and 368(5), stating that any law passed by Parliament could not be challenged in court. The Supreme Court ruled in *Minerva Mills v. Union of India* that judicial review is a basic characteristic of the constitution, overturning Articles 368(4), 368(5) and 31C.

Flexibility

According to Granville Austin, "The Indian constitution is first and foremost a social document, and is aided by its Parts III & IV (Fundamental Rights & Directive Principles of State Policy, respectively) acting together, as its chief instruments and its conscience, in realising the goals set by it for all the people." The constitution has deliberately been worded in generalities (not in vague terms) to ensure its flexibility. John Marshall, the fourth chief justice of the United States, said that a constitution's "great outlines should be marked, its important objects designated, and the minor ingredients which compose those objects be deduced from the nature of the objects themselves." A document "intended to endure for ages to come", it must be interpreted not only based on the intention and understanding of its framers, but in the existing social and political context.

The "right to life" guaranteed under **Article 21**[A] has been expanded to include a number of human rights, including:

- the right to a speedy trial;

- the right to water;

- the right to earn a livelihood,

- the right to health, and

- the right to education.

At the conclusion of his book, *Making of India's Constitution*, retired Supreme Court Justice Hans Raj Khanna wrote:

If the Indian constitution is our heritage bequeathed to us by our founding fathers, no less are we, the people of India, the trustees and custodians of the values which pulsate within its provisions! A constitution is not a parchment of paper, it is a way of life and has to be lived up to. Eternal vigilance is the price of liberty and in the final analysis, its only keepers are the people."

ANNEXURE-III

· ·

PRIME MINISTERS OF INDIA DURING VARIOUS PERIODS

BJP (2)[a] INC/INC(I)/INC(R)[b] (6+1 acting[c]) JD (3) JP (1) JP(S) (1) SJP(R) (1)				
No.	Portrait	Name (Birth–Death)	Constituency	Party (Alliance)
2		Lal Bahadur Shastri (1904–1966)	Allahabad, Uttar Pradesh	Indian National Congress
6		Rajiv Gandhi (1944–1991)	Amethi, Uttar Pradesh	Indian National Congress (I)
6		Rajiv Gandhi (1944–1991)	Amethi, Uttar Pradesh	Indian National Congress (I)
5		Chaudhary Charan Singh (1902–1987)	Baghpat, Uttar Pradesh	Janata Party (Secular)
8		Chandra Shekhar (1927–2007)	Ballia, Uttar Pradesh	Samajwadi Janata Party (Rashtriya) with INC(I)

Term of office[15]			Lok Sabha[d]	Ministry	Appointed by
Took office	Left office	Time in office			
9 June 1964	11 January 1966†	1 year, 216 days	3rd	Shastri I	Sarvepalli Radhakrishnan
31 October 1984	2 December 1989	5 years, 32 days	7th	Rajiv	Zail Singh
31 October 1984	2 December 1989	5 years, 32 days	8th	Rajiv	Zail Singh
28 July 1979	14 January 1980[RES]	170 days	6th	Charan	Neelam Sanjiva Reddy
10 November 1990	21 June 1991[RES]	223 days	9th	Chandra Shekhar	R. Venkataraman

(Contd.)

BJP (2)[a] INC/INC(I)/INC(R)[b] (6+1 acting[c]) JD (3) JP (1) JP(S) (1) SJP(R) (1)				
No.	**Portrait**	**Name (Birth–Death)**	**Constituency**	**Party (Alliance)**
7		Vishwanath Pratap Singh (1931–2008)	Fatehpur, Uttar Pradesh	Janata Dal (National Front)
10		Atal Bihari Vajpayee (1924–2018)	Lucknow, Uttar Pradesh	Bharatiya Janata Party
(10)		Atal Bihari Vajpayee (1924–2018)	Lucknow, Uttar Pradesh	Bharatiya Janata Party (NDA)
(10)		Atal Bihari Vajpayee (1924–2018)	Lucknow, Uttar Pradesh	Bharatiya Janata Party (NDA)

Term of office[15]			Lok Sabha[d]	Ministry	Appointed by
Took office	Left office	Time in office			
2 December 1989	10 November 1990[NC]	343 days	9th	Vishwanath	R. Venkataraman
16 May 1996	1 June 1996[RES]	16 days	11th	Vajpayee I	Shankar Dayal Sharma
19 March 1998[§]	22 May 2004	6 years, 64 days	12th	Vajpayee II	K. R. Narayanan
19 March 1998[§]	22 May 2004	6 years, 64 days	13th	Vajpayee III	K. R. Narayanan

(Contd.)

BJP (2)[a] INC/INC(I)/INC(R)[b] (6+1 acting[c]) JD (3) JP (1) JP(S) (1) SJP(R) (1)				
No.	Portrait	Name (Birth–Death)	Constituency	Party (Alliance)
(3)		Indira Gandhi (1917–1984)	Medak, Andhra Pradesh	Indian National Congress (I)
9		Pamulaparthi Venkata Narasimha Rao (1921–2004)	Nandyal, Andhra Pradesh	Indian National Congress (I)
1		Jawaharlal Nehru (1889–1964)	Phulpur, Uttar Pradesh	Indian National Congress
1		Jawaharlal Nehru (1889–1964)	Phulpur, Uttar Pradesh	Indian National Congress

	Term of office[15]		Lok Sabha[d]	Ministry	Appointed by
Took office	**Left office**	**Time in office**			
14 January 1980[§]	31 October 1984†	4 years, 291 days	7th	Indira III	Neelam Sanjiva Reddy
21 June 1991	16 May 1996	4 years, 330 days	10th	Rao	R. Venkataraman
15 August 1947	27 May 1964†	16 years, 286 days	Constituent Assembly [e]	Nehru I	The Earl Mountbatten of Burma
15 August 1947	27 May 1964†	16 years, 286 days	1st	Nehru II	Rajendra Prasad

(Contd.)

BJP (2)[a] INC/INC(I)/INC(R)[b] (6+1 acting[c]) JD (3) JP (1) JP(S) (1) SJP(R) (1)				
No.	Portrait	Name (Birth–Death)	Constituency	Party (Alliance)
1		Jawaharlal Nehru (1889–1964)	Phulpur, Uttar Pradesh	Indian National Congress
1		Jawaharlal Nehru (1889–1964)	Phulpur, Uttar Pradesh	Indian National Congress
3		Indira Gandhi (1917–1984)	Rae Bareli, Uttar Pradesh	Indian National Congress (R)
3		Indira Gandhi (1917–1984)	Rae Bareli, Uttar Pradesh	Indian National Congress (R)

| Term of office[15] | | | Lok Sabha[d] | Ministry | Appointed by |
Took office	Left office	Time in office			
15 August 1947	27 May 1964†	16 years, 286 days	2nd	Nehru III	Rajendra Prasad
15 August 1947	27 May 1964†	16 years, 286 days	3rd	Nehru IV	Rajendra Prasad
24 January 1966	24 March 1977	11 years, 59 days	4th	Indira I	Sarvepalli Radhakrishnan
24 January 1966	24 March 1977	11 years, 59 days	5th	Indira II	V. V. Giri

(Contd.)

BJP (2)[a] INC/INC(I)/INC(R)[b] (6+1 acting[c]) JD (3) JP (1) JP(S) (1) SJP(R) (1)				
No.	Portrait	Name (Birth–Death)	Constituency	Party (Alliance)
13		Manmohan Singh (1932–)	Rajya Sabha MP for Assam	Indian National Congress (UPA)
13		Manmohan Singh (1932–)	Rajya Sabha MP for Assam	Indian National Congress (UPA)
12		Inder Kumar Gujral (1919–2012)	Rajya Sabha MP for Bihar	Janata Dal (United Front)
11		Haradanahalli Doddegowda Deve Gowda (1933–)	Rajya Sabha MP for Karnataka	Janata Dal (United Front)

| Term of office[15] | | | Lok Sabha[d] | Ministry | Appointed by |
Took office	Left office	Time in office			
22 May 2004	26 May 2014	10 years, 4 days	14th	Manmohan I	A. P. J. Abdul Kalam
22 May 2004	26 May 2014	10 years, 4 days	15th	Manmohan II	Pratibha Patil
21 April 1997	19 March 1998	332 days	11th	Gujral	Shankar Dayal Sharma
1 June 1996	21 April 1997[RES]	324 days	11th	Deve Gowda	Shankar Dayal Sharma

(Contd.)

BJP (2)[a] INC/INC(I)/INC(R)[b] (6+1 acting[c]) JD (3) JP (1) JP(S) (1) SJP(R) (1)				
No.	Portrait	Name (Birth–Death)	Constituency	Party (Alliance)
3		Indira Gandhi (1917–1984)	Rajya Sabha MP for Uttar Pradesh	Indian National Congress
Acting		Gulzarilal Nanda (1898–1998)	Sabarkantha, Gujarat	Indian National Congress
Acting		Gulzarilal Nanda (1898–1998)	Sabarkantha, Gujarat	Indian National Congress
4		Morarji Ranchhodji Desai (1896–1995)	Surat, Gujarat	Janata Party

Term of office[15]			Lok Sabha[d]	Ministry	Appointed by
Took office	Left office	Time in office			
24 January 1966	24 March 1977	11 years, 59 days	3rd	Indira I	Sarvepalli Radhakrishnan
27 May 1964	9 June 1964	13 days	3rd	Nanda I	Sarvepalli Radhakrishnan
11 January 1966	24 January 1966	13 days	3rd	Nanda II	Sarvepalli Radhakrishnan
24 March 1977	28 July 1979[RES]	2 years, 126 days	6th	Desai	B. D. Jatti (acting)

(Contd.)

BJP (2)[a] INC/INC(I)/INC(R)[b] (6+1 acting[c]) JD (3) JP (1) JP(S) (1) SJP(R) (1)				
No.	Portrait	Name (Birth–Death)	Constituency	Party (Alliance)
14		Narendra Modi (1950–)	Varanasi, Uttar Pradesh	Bharatiya Janata Party (NDA)
14		Narendra Modi (1950–)	Varanasi, Uttar Pradesh	Bharatiya Janata Party (NDA)

| | Term of office[15] | | Lok Sabha[d] | Ministry | Appointed by |
Took office	Left office	Time in office			
26 May 2014	Incumbent	6 years, 293 days	16th	Modi I	Pranab Mukherjee
26 May 2014	Incumbent	6 years, 293 days	17th	Modi II	Ram Nath Kovind

Statistics[edit]

List of prime ministers by length of term

No.	Name	Party	Length of term	
			Longest continuous term	**Total years of premiership**
1	Jawaharlal Nehru	INC	16 years, 286 days	16 years, 286 days
2	Indira Gandhi	INC/INC(I)/INC(R)	11 years, 59 days	15 years, 350 days
3	Manmohan Singh	INC	10 years, 4 days	10 years, 4 days
4	**Narendra Modi**	**BJP**	**6 years, 293 days**	**6 years, 293 days**
5	Atal Bihari Vajpayee	BJP	6 years, 64 days	6 years, 80 days
6	Rajiv Gandhi	INC(I)	5 years, 32 days	5 years, 32 days
7	P. V. Narasimha Rao	INC(I)	4 years, 330 days	4 years, 330 days
8	Morarji Desai	JP	2 years, 126 days	2 years, 126 days
9	Lal Bahadur Shastri	INC	1 year, 216 days	1 year, 216 days
10	Vishwanath Pratap Singh	JD	343 days	343 days
11	Inder Kumar Gujral	JD	332 days	332 days

No.	Name	Party	Length of term	
			Longest continuous term	Total years of premiership
12	H. D. Deve Gowda	JD	324 days	324 days
13	Chandra Shekhar	SJP(R)	223 days	223 days
14	Charan Singh	JP(S)	170 days	170 days

ANNEXURE-IV

https://en.wikipedia.org/wiki/Scheduled_Castes_and_Scheduled_Tribes

SCHEDULED CASTES AND SCHEDULED TRIBES OF INDIA

The Scheduled Caste (SCs) and Scheduled Tribes (STs) are officially designated groups of people in India. The terms are recognised in the Constitution of India and the groups are designated in one or other of the categories. For much of the period of British rule in the Indian subcontinent, they were known as the Depressed Classes. In modern literature, the Scheduled Castes are sometimes referred to as Dalit, meaning **"broken/scattered"** in Sanskrit, having been popularised by **B. R. Ambedkar** (1891–1956), the economist, reformer, chairman of the Constitution assembly of India, and Dalit leader during the independence struggle, himself a Dalit. Ambedkar preferred the term Dalit to Gandhi's term, Harijan, meaning "person of Hari/Vishnu" (or Man of God). In September 2018, the government "issued an advisory to all private satellite channels asking them to 'refrain' from using the nomenclature 'Dalit'", though "rights groups and intellectuals have come out against any shift from 'Dalit' in popular usage". The Scheduled Castes and Scheduled Tribes comprise about 16.6% and 8.6%, respectively, of India's population (according to the 2011 census). The Constitution (Scheduled Castes) Order, 1950 lists 1,108 castes across 28 states in its First Schedule, and the Constitution (Scheduled Tribes) Order, 1950 lists 744 tribes across 22 states in its First Schedule. Since the independence of India, the Scheduled Castes and Scheduled Tribes were given Reservation status, guaranteeing political representation. The Constitution lays down the general principles of positive discrimination for SCs and STs.

- The Constitution provides a three-pronged strategy to improve the situation of SCs and STs:

- *Protective arrangements:* Such measures as are required to enforce equality, to provide punitive measures for transgressions, and to eliminate established practices that perpetuate inequities. A number of laws were enacted to implement the provisions in the Constitution. Examples of such laws include the Untouchability Practices Act, 1955, Scheduled Caste and Scheduled Tribe (Prevention of Atrocities) Act, 1989, The Employment of Manual Scavengers and Construction of Dry Latrines (Prohibition) Act, 1993, etc. Despite legislation, social discrimination and atrocities against the backward castes continued to persist.[18]

- *Affirmative action:* Provide positive treatment in allotment of jobs and access to higher education as a means to accelerate the integration of the SCs and STs with mainstream society. Affirmative action is popularly known as reservation. Article 16 of the Constitution states "nothing in this article shall prevent the State from making any provisions for the reservation of appointments or posts in favor of any backward class of citizens, which, in the opinion of the state, is not adequately represented in the services under the State". The Supreme Court upheld the legality of affirmative action and the Mandal Commission (a report that recommended that affirmative action not only apply to the Untouchables, but the other backward castes as well). However, the reservations from affirmative action were only allotted in the public sector, not the private.[19]

- *Development:* Provide resources and benefits to bridge the socioeconomic gap between the SCs and STs and other communities. Major part played by the Hidayatullah National Law University. Legislation to improve the socioeconomic situation of SCs and STs because twenty-seven percent of SC and thirty-seven percent of ST households lived below the poverty line, compared to the mere eleven percent among other households. Additionally, the backward castes were poorer than other groups in Indian society, and they suffered from higher morbidity and mortality rates.

- The Indian constitution, in Constitution (Scheduled Castes) Order, 1950 lists 1,108 castes across 25 states in its First Schedule, while the Constitution (**Scheduled Tribes**) Order, 1950 lists 744 tribes across 22 states in its First Schedule.

ANNEXURE-V

SCHEDULED CASTES IN INDIA

The evolution of low castes to modern-day Scheduled Castes is complex. The caste system as a stratification of classes in India originated about 2,000 years ago, and has been influenced by dynasties and ruling elites including the Mughal Empire and the British Raj. The Hindu concept of Varna historically incorporated occupation-based communities.

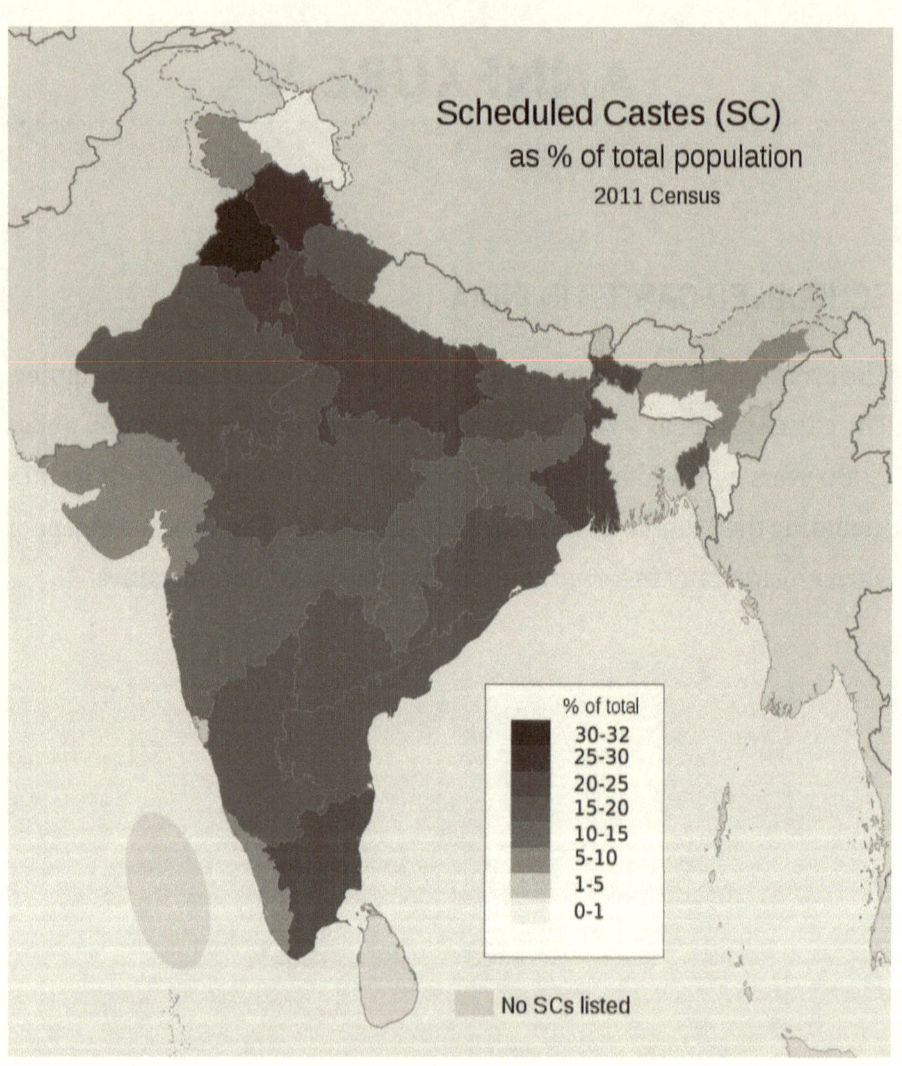

Wikipedia · Text under CC-BY-SA license

By M Tracy Hunter - Own work, CC BY-SA 3.0, https://commons. wikimedia.org/w/index.php?curid=33731323

Schedules Caste Population by State

States with population of Scheduled Castes as per 2011 census[28]			
State	**Population**	**Scheduled Caste (%)**	**Scheduled Caste Population**
India	**1,210,854,977**	**16.63**	**201,378,086**
Andhra Pradesh	84,580,777	16.41	13,878,078
Arunachal Pradesh	1,383,727	0.00	0
Assam	31,205,576	7.15	2,231,321
Bihar	104,099,452	15.91	16,567,325
Chhattisgarh	25,545,198	12.82	3,274,269
Goa	1,458,545	1.74	25,449
Gujarat	60,439,692	6.74	4,074,447
Haryana	25,351,462	20.17	5,113,615
Himachal Pradesh	6,864,602	25.19	1,729,252
Jammu & Kashmir	12,541,302	7.38	924,991
Jharkhand	32,988,134	12.08	3,985,644
Karnataka	61,095,297	17.15	10,474,992
Kerala	33,406,061	9.10	3,039,573
Madhya Pradesh	72,626,809	15.62	11,342,320
Maharashtra	112,374,333	11.81	13,275,898
Manipur	2,570,390	3.78	97,042
Meghalaya	2,966,889	0.58	17,355
Mizoram	10,97,206	0.11	1,218
Nagaland	1,978,502	0.00	0
Odisha	41,974,218	17.13	71,88,463
Punjab	27,743,338	31.94	8,860,179
Rajasthan	68,548,437	17.83	12,221,593
Sikkim	610,577	4.63	28,275

(Contd.)

States with population of Scheduled Castes as per 2011 census[28]			
State	**Population**	**Scheduled Caste (%)**	**Scheduled Caste Population**
Tamil Nadu	72,147,030	20.01	14,438,445
Tripura	3,673,917	17.83	654,918
Uttar Pradesh	199,812,341	20.70	41,357,608
Uttarakhand	10,086,292	18.76	1,892,516
West Bengal	91,276,115	23.51	21,463,270

ANNEXURE-VI

Tribal Welfare And Development

The term 'Scheduled Tribes' first appeared in the Constitution of India. Article 366 (25) defined scheduled tribes as "such tribes or tribal communities or parts of or groups within such tribes or tribal communities as are deemed under Article 342 to be Scheduled Tribes for the purposes of this constitution". Article 342, which is reproduced below, prescribes procedure to be followed in the matter of specification of scheduled tribes.

Article 342

The President may, with respect to any State or Union territory, and where it is a state, after consultation with the Governor there of by public notification, specify the tribes or tribal communities or parts of or groups within tribes or tribal communities which shall, for the purposes of this constitution, is deemed to be scheduled tribes in relation to that state or Union Territory, as the case may be.

Parliament may by law include in or exclude from the list of Scheduled tribes specified in a notification issued under clause(1) any tribe or tribal community or part of or group within any tribe or tribal community, but save as aforesaid, a notification issued under the said clause shall not be varied by any subsequent notification.

Thus, the first specification of Scheduled Tribes in relation to a particular State/Union Territory is by a notified order of the President, after consultation with the State governments concerned. These orders can be modified subsequently only through an Act of Parliament. The above Article also provides for listing of scheduled tribes State/Union Territory wise and not on an all India basis.

The criterion followed for specification of a community, as scheduled tribes are indications of primitive traits, distinctive culture, geographical isolation, shyness of contact with the community at large, and backwardness. This criterion is not spelt out in the Constitution but has become well established. It subsumes the definitions contained in 1931Census, the reports of first Backward Classes Commission 1955, the Advisory Committee (Kalelkar), on Revision of SC/ST lists (Lokur Committee), 1965 and the Joint Committee of Parliament on the Scheduled Castes and Scheduled Tribes orders (Amendment) Bill 1967 (Chanda Committee), 1969.

The list of Scheduled Tribes is State/UT specific and a community declared as a Scheduled Tribe in a State need not be so in another State. The inclusion of a community as a Scheduled Tribe is an ongoing process.

The essential characteristics of these communities are:

- Primitive Traits

- Geographical isolation

- Distinct culture

- Shy of contact with community at large

- Economically backward

Tribal communities live, in various ecological and geo-climatic conditions ranging from plains and forests to hills and inaccessible areas. Tribal groups are at different stages of social, economic and educational development. While some tribal communities have adopted a mainstream way of life, at the other end of the spectrum, there are certain Scheduled Tribes, 75 in number known as Particularly Vulnerable Tribal Groups (PVTGs), who are characterised by

- pre-agriculture level of technology

- stagnant or declining population

- extremely low literacy

- subsistence level of economy

The Scheduled Tribes are notified in 30 States/UTs and the number of individual ethnic groups, etc. notified as Scheduled Tribes is 705. The tribal population of the country, as per 2011 census, is 10.43 crore, constituting 8.6% of the total population. 89.97% of them live in rural areas and 10.03% in urban areas. The decadal population growth of the tribal's from Census 2001 to 2011 has been 23.66% against the 17.69% of the entire population. The sex ratio for the overall population is 940 females per 1000 males and that of Scheduled Tribes 990 females per thousand males.

- Broadly the STs inhabit two distinct geographical area – the Central India and the North- Eastern Area. More than half of the Scheduled Tribe population is concentrated in Central

India, i.e., Madhya Pradesh (14.69%), Chhattisgarh (7.5%), Jharkhand (8.29%), Andhra Pradesh (5.7%), Maharashtra (10.08%), Orissa (9.2%), Gujarat (8.55%) and Rajasthan (8.86%). The other distinct area is the North East (Assam, Nagaland, Mizoram, Manipur, Meghalaya, Tripura, Sikkim and Arunachal Pradesh).

- More than two-third of the ST population is concentrated only in the seven States of the country, viz. Madhya Pradesh, Maharashtra, Orissa, Gujarat, Rajasthan, Jharkhand and Chhattisgarh. There is no ST population in 3 States (Delhi NCR, Punjab and Haryana) and 2 UTs (Puducherry and Chandigarh), as no Scheduled Tribe is notified.

Literacy rate

The progress over the years on the literacy front may be seen from the following:

	1961	1971	1981	1991	2001	2011
Total literate population	24 %	29.4 %	36.2 %	52.2 %	64.84%	73.00 %
Scheduled Tribes (STs) population	8.5 %	11.3 %	16.3 %	29.6 %	47.10%	59.00%
Total female population	12.9 %	18.6 %	29.8 %	39.3 %	53.67%	64.60%
Total Scheduled Tribes (STs) female population	3.2 %	4.8 %	8.0 %	18.2 %	34.76%	49.40 %

Source: *Ministry of Tribal Affairs*

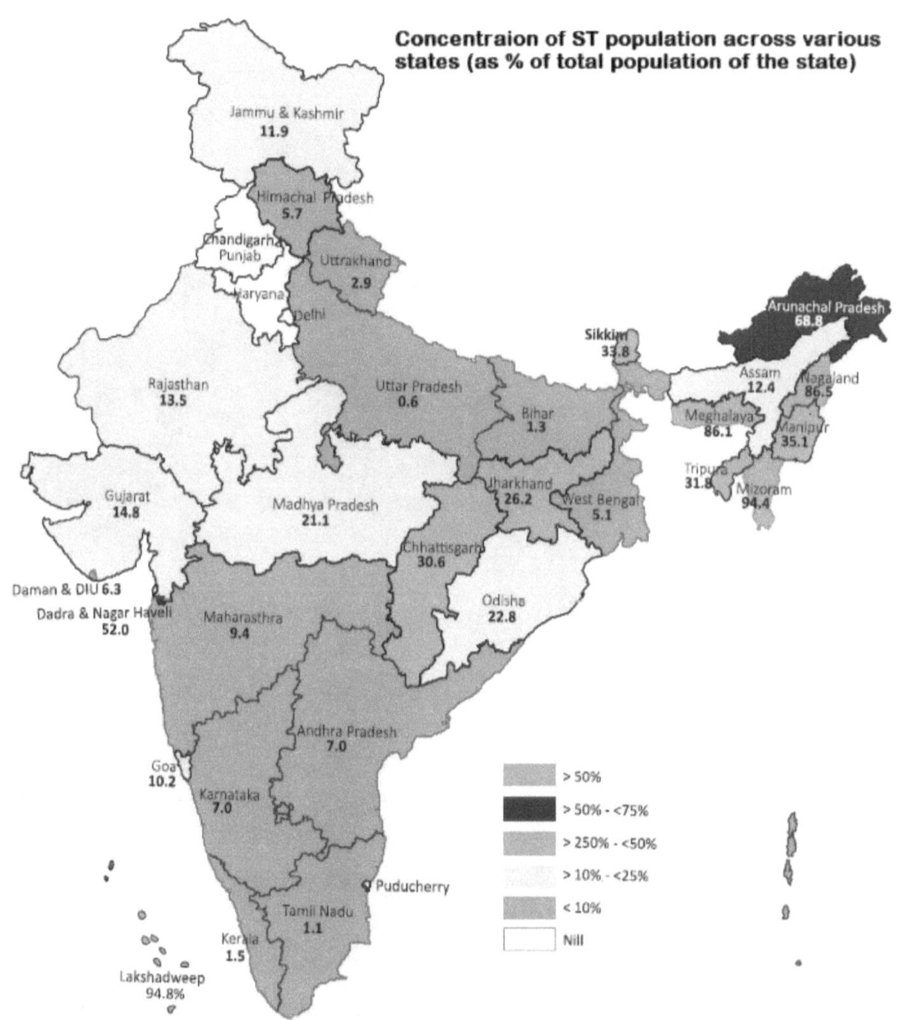

Concentraion of ST population across various states (as % of total population of the state)
Jammu & Kashmir
11.9
Himachal Pradesh
5.7
Chandigarh
Punjab
Uttrakhand
2.9
Haryana
Delhi
Rajasthan
13.5
Uttar Pradesh
0.6
Sikkim
33.8
Arunachal Pradesh
68.8
Assam
12.4
Nagaland
86.5
Bihar
1.3
Meghalaya
86.1
Manipur
35.1
Gujarat
14.8
Madhya Pradesh
21.1
Jharkhand
26.2
West Bengal
5.1
Tripura
31.8
Mizoram
94.4
Chhattisgarh
30.6
Daman & DIU 6.3
Dadra & Nagar Haveli
52.0
Maharasthra
9.4
Odisha
22.8
Andhra Pradesh
7.0
Goa
10.2
Karnataka
7.0
Puducherry
Tamil Nadu
1.1
Kerala
1.5
Lakshadweep
94.8%
> 50%
> 50% - <75%
> 250% - <50%
> 10% - <25%
< 10%
Nill

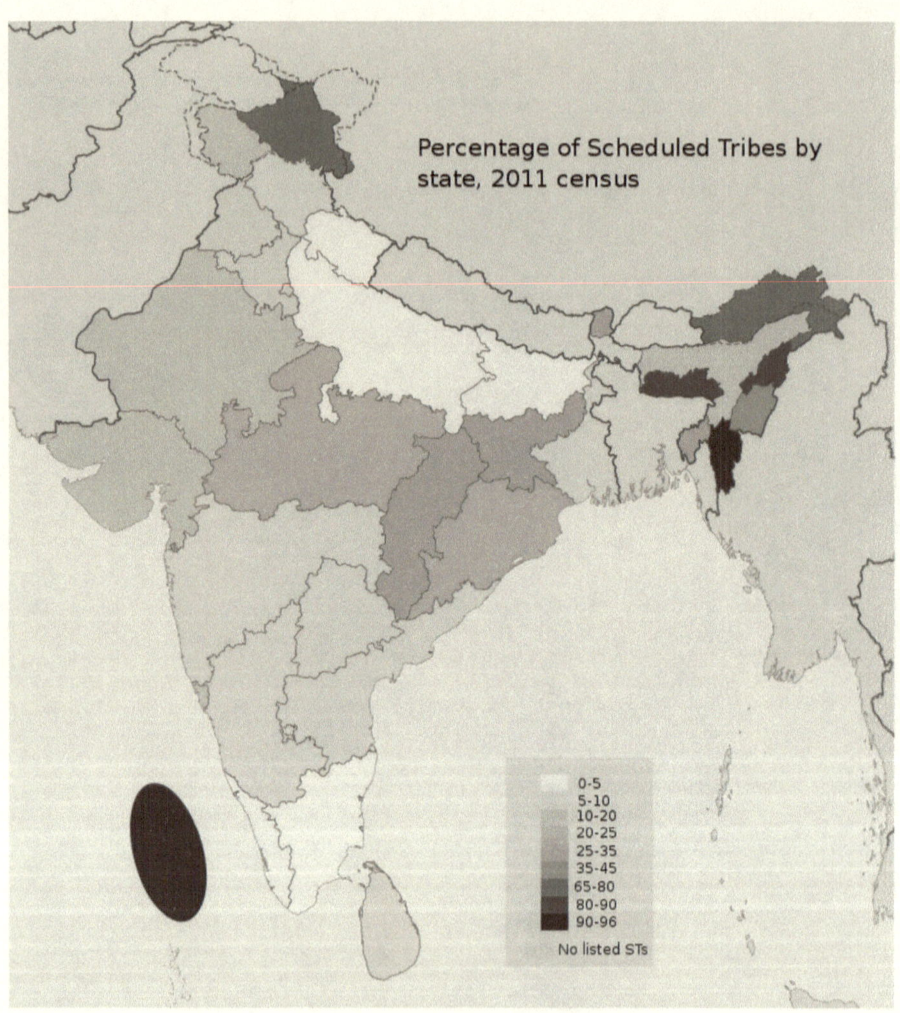

By M Tracy Hunter - Own work, CC BY-SA 3.0, https://commons.
wikimedia.org/w/index.php?curid=33732550

Scheduled Tribe Population by State

States with population of Scheduled Tribes as per 2011 census			
State	**Population**	**Scheduled Tribe (%)**	**Scheduled Tribe Population**
India	**1,210,854,977**	**8.61**	**104,254,613**
Andhra Pradesh	84,580,777	7.00	5,920,654
Arunachal Pradesh	1,383,727	68.79	951,865
Assam	31,205,576	12.45	3,885,094
Bihar	104,099,452	1.28	1,332,472
Chhattisgarh	25,545,198	30.62	7,821,939
Goa	1,458,545	10.21	148,917
Gujarat	60,439,692	14.75	8,914,854
Haryana	25,351,462	0.00	0
Himachal Pradesh	6,864,602	5.71	391,968
Jammu & Kashmir	12,541,302	11.90	1,492,414
Jharkhand	32,988,134	26.21	8,646,189
Karnataka	61,095,297	6.95	4,246,123
Kerala	33,406,061	1.45	484,387
Madhya Pradesh	72,626,809	21.09	15,316,994
Maharashtra	112,374,333	9.35	10,507,000
Manipur	2,570,390	35.14	903,235
Meghalaya	2,966,889	86.15	2,555,974
Mizoram	1,097,206	94.44	1,036,201
Nagaland	1,978,502	86.46	1,710,612
Odisha	41,974,218	22.85	9,591,108
Punjab	27,743,338	0.00	0
Rajasthan	68,548,437	13.48	9,240,329
Sikkim	610,577	33.72	205,886

(Contd.)

States with population of Scheduled Tribes as per 2011 census			
State	**Population**	**Scheduled Tribe (%)**	**Scheduled Tribe Population**
Tamil Nadu	72,147,030	1.10	793,617
Tripura	3,673,917	31.76	1,166,836
Uttar Pradesh	199,812,341	0.57	1,138,930
Uttarakhand	10,086,292	2.90	292,502
West Bengal	91,276,115	5.80	5,294,014

The Tribal people are also known as Adivasis. The word Adivasi means the first inhabitants or the Indigenous People, a phrase recognised by the Supreme Court of India. They comprise a substantial indigenous minority of the population of India. Adivasi societies are particularly prominent in Andhra Pradesh, Chhattisgarh, Gujarat, Jharkhand, Madhyapradesh, Maharashtra, Odisha, West Bengal, and some north-eastern states, and the Andaman and Nicobar Islands. Many smaller tribal groups are quite sensitive to ecological degradation caused by modernisation. Both commercial forestry and intensive agriculture have proved destructive to the forests that had endured swidden agriculture for many centuries. Adivasis in central part of India have been victims of the Salwa Judum campaign by the Government against the Naxalite insurgency. More than half of the Scheduled Tribes population is concentrated in 6 States viz. Madhya Pradesh, Chhattisgarh, Maharashtra, Orissa, Jharkhand and Gujarat. Tribal communities live in about 15% of the total geographical area of the country.

The governmental programmes implemented in India for the uplift and rehabilitation of tribals has not been able to achieve their goals.

The strategies adopted by the British administrators for solving the problems of the tribals included acquiring tribal land and forests and declaring certain tribal areas as excluded or partially excluded. But, the British government had also established a number of schools and hospitals in the tribal areas with the help of Christian missionaries who converted many tribals to Christianity. Thus, by and large, during the British period, the tribals remained victims of colonial-feudal domination, ethnic prejudices, illiteracy, poverty, and isolation. After Independence, provisions were made in the Constitution to safeguard tribal interests and promote their developmental and welfare activities. Article 366(25) of the Constitution of India refers to Scheduled Tribes as those communities, who are scheduled in accordance with the Article 342 of the Constitution.

Constitutional Safeguards

The Constitution has devoted more than 20 articles on the redressal and upliftment of the underprivileged following the policy of positive discrimination and affirmative action, particularly with reference to the Scheduled Tribes. Recognising the special needs of STs, the Constitution of India made certain special safeguards to protect these communities from all the possible exploitation and thus ensure social justice. While Article 14 confers equal rights and opportunities to all, Article 15 prohibits discrimination against any citizen on the grounds of sex, religion, race, caste etc; Article 15 (4) enjoins upon the State to make special provisions for the advancement of any socially and educationally backward classes; Article 16 (4) empowers the State to make provisions for reservation in appointments or posts in favour of any backward class of citizens, which in the opinion of the State, is not adequately represented in the services under the State; Article 46 enjoins upon the State to promote with special care the educational and economic interests of the weaker sections of the people and, in particular, the STs and promises to protect them from social injustice and all forms of exploitation. Further, while Article 275 (1) promises grant-in-aid for promoting the welfare of STs and for raising the level of administration of the Scheduled Areas, Articles 330, 332 and 335 stipulate reservation of seats for STs in the Lok Sabha and in the State Legislative Assemblies and in services. Finally, the Constitution also empowers the State to appoint a Commission to investigate the conditions of the socially and educationally backward classes (Article 340) and to specify those Tribes or Tribal Communities deemed to be as STs (Article 342).

The Fifth Schedule to the Constitution lays down certain prescriptions about the Scheduled Areas as well as the Scheduled Tribes in States other than Assam, Meghalaya, Tripura and Mizoram by ensuring submission of Annual Reports by the Governors to the President of India regarding the Administration of the Scheduled Areas and setting up of Tribal Advisory Councils to advise on matters pertaining to the welfare and advancement of the STs (Article 244(1)). Likewise, the Sixth Schedule to the Constitution also refers to the administration of Tribal Areas in the states of Assam, Meghalaya, Tripura and Mizoram by designating certain tribal areas as Autonomous Districts and Autonomous Regions and also by constituting District Councils and Regional Councils (Article 244(2)). To ensure effective participation of the tribes in the process of planning and decision-making, the 73rd and 74th Amendments of the Constitution extend to the Scheduled Areas through the Panchayats (Extension to the Scheduled Areas) Act, 1996.

Representation in Legislatures and Panchayats

The Constitution of India prescribes protection and safeguards for Scheduled Tribes with the object of promoting their educational and economic interests. Under Article 330 and 332 of the Indian Constitution, seats have been reserved for Scheduled Tribes in Lok Sabha and state Vidhan Sabhas. Following the introduction of Panchayati Raj, Suitable safeguards have been provided for proper representation" of the members of the Scheduled Tribes by reserving seats for them in the Gram Panchayats, Block Panchayats, District Panchayats etc.

Reservation in the Service

The government has made provisions for their adequate representation in the services.

To facilitate their adequate representation certain concessions have been provided, such as:

i. Exemption in age limits,

ii. Relaxation in the standard of suitability

iv. Inclusion at least in the lower category for the purpose of promotion is otherwise than through qualifying examinations.

Administration of Scheduled and Tribal Areas

'Scheduled Areas' have been declared in the States of Andhra Pradesh, Bihar, Gujarat, Madhya Pradesh, Maharashtra, Orissa, Himachal Pradesh and Rajasthan. The scheme of administration of' Scheduled Areas under the Fifth Schedule visualises a division of responsibility between the State and Union Governments. The State Governments have been given the responsibility of screening the legislations which are unsuitable for extension to the tribal areas. They are also responsible for framing rules for the prevention of exploitation of the tribes by the moneylenders. They implement schemes for the welfare of the tribes living within its boundary.

The Union Government provides guidelines in regard to the administration of Scheduled Areas. It also provides necessary funds that are required to raise the standard of administration and for the improvement in the quality of life of the tribal communities. The Union Government also has the power to give directions to the State Governments about matters relating to the welfare of the Scheduled Tribes.

Development Plans

High priority to the welfare and development of STs has been given right from the beginning of the first five-year plan. The First Five Year Plan (1951-56) clearly laid down the principle stating that 'the general development programs should be so designed to cater adequately for the backward classes and special provisions should be used for securing additional and more intensified development for STs'. Unfortunately, the same could not take place. The Second Plan (1956-61), which lay emphasis oeconomic development, gave a special focus on reducing economic inequalities in the society. Further, development programmes for STs have been planned for, based on respect and understanding of their culture and traditions and with an appreciation of their social, psychological and economic problems. In fact, the same was planned in tune with 'Panchasheel' – the philosophy of tribal development as enunciated by the first Prime Minister of the Country,

Pandit Jawaharlal Nehru. An important landmark during the Second Plan was the opening of 43 Special Multipurpose Tribal Blocks, later termed as Tribal Development Blocks (TDBs). The Third Plan (1961-66) continued with the very same principle of advocating a reduction in inequalities through various policies and programs to provide equality of opportunity to STs. The Fourth Plan (1969-74) proclaimed that the 'basic goal was to realise a rapid increase in the standard of living of the people through measures which also promote 'equality and social justice'. An important step in this direction was setting up of six pilot projects in Andhra Pradesh, Bihar, Madhya Pradesh and Orissa in 1971-72 with a separate Tribal Development Agency for each project. The Fifth Plan (1974-78) marked a shift in approach as reflected in the launching of the Tribal Sub-Plan (TSP) for the direct benefit of the development of tribals. The Tribal Sub-Plan has a two pronged strategy, namely i) promotion of development activities to raise the level of living standards of Scheduled Tribes and ii) protection of their interest through legal and administrative support. The TSP stipulated that funds of the centre and the states should be quantified on the population proportion basis with budgetary mechanisms to ensure accountability, non-divertability and utilisation for the welfare and development of STs.

The Sixth Plan (1980-85) sought to ensure a higher degree of devolution of funds so that at least 50 percent of tribal families could be provided assistance to cross the poverty line. In the Seventh Plan (1985-90), there was a substantial increase in the flow of funds for the development of STs resulting in the expansion of infrastructural facilities and enlargement of coverage. Emphasis was laid on the educational development of STs. For the economic development of STs, two national-level institutions were set up viz. (i) Tribal Cooperative

Marketing Development Federation (TRIFED) in 1987 as an apex body for State Tribal Development Cooperative Corporations, and (ii) National Scheduled Castes and Scheduled Tribes Finance and Development Corporation (NSFDC) in 1989. The former was assigned to provide remunerative prices for the forest and agriculture produce of tribal, while the latter was intended to provide credit support for employment generation.

In the Eighth Plan (1992-97), efforts were intensified to bridge the gap between the levels of development of STs and the other sections of the society. The Plan not only emphasized the elimination of exploitation, but also paid attention to the special problems of suppression of rights, land alienation, non-payment of minimum wages and restrictions on the right to collect minor forest produce etc. However, attention on priority basis was continued to be paid on the socio-economic upliftment of STs.

The Ninth Plan (1997-2002) aimed to empower STs by creating an enabling environment conducive for them to exercise their rights freely, enjoy their privileges and lead a life of self-confidence and dignity, on par with the rest of society. This process essentially encompassed three vital components, viz. i) Social Empowerment; ii) Economic Empowerment; and iii) Social justice. To this effect, while ST-related line Ministries/Departments implemented general development policies and programmes, the nodal Ministry of Tribal Affairs implemented certain ST-specific innovative programmes.

The Tenth Plan approach to the tribal development focused on tackling the unresolved issues and problems on a time bound basis, besides providing adequate space and opportunity for the tribes to empower themselves with the strength of their own potentials.

The Eleventh Plan attempted a paradigm shift with respect to the overall empowerment of the tribals keeping the issues related to the governance at the centre. The operational imperatives of the Vth Schedule, TSP 1976, PESA 1996, RFRA 2006; the desirability of a tribal-centric, tribal participative and tribal-managed development process, and the need for a conscious departure from dependence on a largely under effective official delivery system will be kept in view during this shift. After the Fifth Five Year Plan, the Tribal Sub-Plan (TSP) strategy was designed in 1980 which consisted of two things: (I) socioeconomic development of the STs, and (ii) Protection oftribess against exploitation. The funds for TSPs are provided by state governments and the central ministries.

However, TSP results were not commensurate with the expectations and the investments made so far as heavy emphasis is laid in several states on infrastructural development without a corresponding emphasis on the development of the STs. The TSP schemes are supposed to lay emphasis on family-oriented income-generating schemes in sectors like agriculture, animal husbandry, cooperatives, tribal crafts and skills, etc., besides laying emphasis on education, health, and housing. In the Five Year Plans, the programmes for the welfare of the STs aim at:

1. Raising the productivity levels in agriculture, animal husbandry, forestry, cottage and small-scale industries, etc., to improve the economic conditions;

2. Rehabilitation of the bonded labour;

3. Education and training programmes, and

4. Special development programmes for women and children.

But various evaluation studies on all these programmes for the integrated development of the tribals have brought out the inadequacies of these programmes.

ANNEXURE-VII

Prof. (Dr) D. Swaminadhan

Profile

Prof. (Dr) D. Swaminadhan

Ph.D. (England), D.Sc.(h.c.)., Ph.D(h/c), FIE, FNAE,
FAPAS, MISTE, MISCA.

Residence:

H.No. 8-2-293/82/LP/6,
Lotus Pond Colony, Road No.12,
Banjara Hills, Hyderabad 500 034,
A.P., INDIA
Tel:91-40-23304946
Mobile: 9849150190
Email : swami@ap.nic.in
dsdsrf@gmail.com

PART-I

ACHIEVEMENTS OF PROF. DR. D. SWAMINADHAN

General Background

Prof. Dr. D. Swaminadhan, born on 01/02/1938 at Guntur, Andhra Pradesh, India, formerly a Member, Planning Commission, New Delhi, is a distinguished Engineer, Technologist, Educationist, Researcher, a planner, and a Human Rights crusader. He belongs to the Scheduled Tribes Community and is a first-generation learner. Dr. Swaminadhan spent more than Fifty-five years of his life in higher education, engineering and technological education and Research, educational Planning, and administration with a sound academic foundation. He is a B.E. in Civil Engineering from Andhra University and a Doctorate in Structural engineering from Liverpool University, U.K. His contributions to engineering and technology are well recognized. He is a Fellow of the Institution of Engineers (India) and a Fellow of the Indian National Academy of Engineering. He researched "Articulated Cellular Bridge Decks" and produced a new method of analysis known as the 'Finite element - grillage method' during his research work at the University of Liverpool. He has a flair for 'social action' to improve the quality of life of the poor and women through economic and social empowerment. Hence, he established the Dr. D. Swaminadhan Research Foundation for this purpose. He has projected his ideas through many papers presented and speeches delivered at national and international levels covering areas like sustainable development, environmental protection, urban development, rural development, Value education, social empowerment, women's empowerment, aged, children, and other weaker sections of the society with the underlying thread of Human Rights protection.Dr.Swaminadhan has published a book titled "Selected Speeches of Dr.D.Swaminadhan."The book covers a wide range of disciplines ranging from socio-cultural development to the tools of economic growth like higher education, technical education, environment, science, and engineering and technology.

Addl.Secretary, University Grants Commission (U.G.C.)

During his tenure in the University Grants Commission, he actively involved himself directly and through several Committees. He was a Member of the moulding of the progressive and innovative educational schemes, programs, and approaches. His association with modern academic concepts such as distance education, continuing education, and education through electronic media gave him a futuristic perspective. His exposure in the University Grants Commission provided him with an overview of higher education in the country in general and being a highly qualified Engineer himself, of higher technological education in particular. In addition to this, he had a clear foresight about the dynamics of the development of higher and technical education - a rare combination of conceptual clarity and pragmatic methodology.

Vice-Chancellor, Jawaharlal Nehru Technological University (J.N.T.U.)

Dr. Swaminadhan's tenure as Vice-Chancellor of Jawaharlal Nehru Technological University, Hyderabad, was full of contributions and achievements. The Ten Year Perspective Plan, a meticulously prepared document for the growth of the University, bears ample testimony to his sagacious Planning. He took upon himself the task of developing the University into one of the Centres of excellence, in which job he succeeded admirably. Aware of the primordial place of engineering and technology in India's economic development, he had visualized the University's Mission in terms of excellence and modernization of engineering and technological education and epitomized it in a brochure "The Vision of Mission". He provided a strong nucleus for the University in establishing ten schools of excellence, around which the University was expected to grow. He gave a thrust to the distance education in Engineering and Technology. The University is the first in the country to offer under-graduate and post-graduate programmes in Engineering and Technology through distance education mode. He initiated a project for establishing a National Academy of Pedagogy in Engineering, Technology and Management at the University and the All India Council for Technical Education (A.I.C.T.E.) has approved it in principle.

Member, Planning Commission, Government of India

Keeping in view Dr. Swaminadhan's contributions and achievements in Higher education and in Engineering, Technological and Management education, the Government of India appointed him as Member, Planning Commission, when he was working as Vice-Chancellor of J.N.T. University. His ideas and vision were reflected in the development of nationally important sectors of Higher education, Technical education, Housing, Urban Development, Water Supply and Sanitation during the Eighth Five Year Plan. His initiative in organising a 'Brain storming session on the higher education' in the Planning Commission provided the needed directions and perspectives for the development of higher education during the Eighth Plan.

He stimulated thinking and discussion on making the prestigious Indian Institutes of Technology and Indian Institutes of Management to reorient their activities for national development in the present changed economic scenario in the country. As a result, an Approach Paper was developed by I.I.T.s focusing on new Thrust Areas, International Consultancy, Creation of Corpus Fund and Industrial Foundation. As a sequel, the I.I.T.s and IISc. Bangalore, together proposed focused Technology Development Missions in certain areas of strategic significance and export potential.

He was the Chairman of the National Steering Committee on these Technology Development Missions. Similarly, the IIMs, as the leading and internationally known management institutes, not only identified some vital issues and crucial areas which would contribute towards strengthening management education, Research and training in the country, but also identified certain priority areas which will help them to play a systemic role in the 90's. A Brain Storming Session on Regional Engineering Colleges resulted in the preparation of an Approach document titled "Perspectives for Excellence in Regional Engineering Colleges". Similar brain storming exercises have been initiated on the Polytechnic education and the Technical Teachers Training Institutes (T.T.T.I.s), resulting in similar documents on perspectives for excellence.

As competitiveness in technology requires a high level of scientific capability too, he organised and chaired a brain storming session on "Mathematical Sciences" as well in the Planning Commission. In the context of the changed scenario of globalisation, we need a strong knowledge and information base. Keeping this requirement and also the resources crunch situation in view, he organised and chaired a brain storming session on "Sharing of Library and Information Resources through Networking" in the Planning Commission. Another brain storming session was organised under his Chairmanship, inviting eminent scientists, vice-chancellors and researchers to introspect and to prepare an approach paper on "Strengthening Research Excellence in India".

Dr. Swaminadhan was the Chairman of the following Ninth Plan Steering Committees constituted by the Planning Commission: (i) Steering Committee for Education Sector - University Education open learning system and technical and management education; (ii) Steering Committee on Urban Infrastructure, Housing and Urban Poverty; and (iii) Steering Committee on Rural Water Supply, Sanitation and Housing.

Value-orientation of Education

Dr. Swaminadhan took keen interest in the most crucial areas of Value Orientation of Education. He took the much needed initiative towards constituting a Planning Commission Core Group on Value Orientation of Education to consider the role of Value education in the entire educational system, to review the existing arrangements and programmes and to formulate concrete programmes for development of value education for all stages of education and to suggest various models and modalities for implementation. For the first time in the history of Educational Policy and Planning in India, Dr. Swaminadhan took the lead in the areas of Value Education which will contribute to the growth of an integrated personality among the new generation who will be leaders in all walks of life. As in the case of higher education, management and technological education - where new ground has been covered, in the area of Value Orientation of Education too, Dr. Swaminadhan proposes to initiate the much needed transformation of education, promoting national integration and international understanding. He was the Chairman of the Standing Committee on Value Orientation of Education constituted by the Ministry of Human Resources Development.

Swaminadhan Model

Dr. Swaminadhan's contributions to University-Industry Interaction and University-Industry - R & D Laboratories - Professional Bodies and Academies interaction have been well recognised through his models; (I) Swaminadhan Model for University-Industry Symbiosis; (II) Swaminadhan Model for University-Industry-R&D Organisation Symbiosis, (III)

Swaminadhan Model for University-Industry-National R&D Laboratories-Professional Bodies and Scientific Academies Interaction for country's economic development. He was the Chairman of the Standing Committee on University – Industry – R & D Labs – Professional Bodies and Scientific Academies interaction, constituted by the Planning Commission.

Dr. D. Swaminadhan Research Foundation

Dr. Swaminadhan is the founder Chairman of "Dr. D. Swaminadhan Research Foundation", a public charitable trust and a registered society with the main objective of contributing towards the advancement of human development based on eco-friendly, pro-poor and gender equity approaches through involving dedicated scientists, technologists, social scientists and social workers in undertaking relevant education, Research, training and innovations for voluntary social action. The Foundation has established the Mahatma Gandhi National Institute of Research and Social Action (MGNIRSA) at Hyderabad to act as an academic and scientific back up support in fulfilling the objectives of the Foundation. The Foundation also established two other Research Institutes: 1. Jawaharlal Nehru Institute of Advanced Studies (J.N.I.A.S.) and 2. Jawaharlal Nehru Institute of Advanced Medical Research (J.N.I.A.M.E.R.) He is the President of all its Institutes.

As a part of the Golden Jubilee Celebrations of the Indian Independence, he organised (through joint collaboration between N.I.R.S.A. & N.I.S.I.E.T. at Hyderabad), a National Seminar on "Fifty years of Indian Independence – Indian Ethos and Human Values: Retrospect & Prospect" in October 1997. As an outcome of the Seminar, M.G.N.I.R.S.A. has established an "International Research Centre for Indian Freedom Movement and National Reconstruction (IRECIFMANAR)", with a view to promote national spirit and work towards National Reconstruction involving freedom fighters, intellectuals, non-resident Indians and others and to promote international understanding, peace, progress and human values.

UNESCO Chair professor

Dr. Swaminadhan has been the UNESCO Chair professor in M.G.N.I.R.S.A. As UNESCO professor, he initiated UNESCO Regional University – Industry Partnership programme (IND – U.N.I.S.P.A.R. Programme) linking up six universities in the South India to undertake specific activities related to University – Industry interaction.

UNESCO International Consultant

Dr. Swaminadhan was sent to Kathmandu, Nepal by UNESCO as an UNESCO International Consultant as a part of its Technical support to the Ministry of Science & Technology (MOST), His Majesty's Government of Nepal in formulating its New Science & Technology policy. He successfully completed the assignment in Dec.1997 – Jan.1998 and submitted the New Science & Technology policy of Nepal document.

Member, National Advisory Council (N.A.C.), Government of India

Recognising his eminence he has been appointed as the Member, National Advisory Council (N.A.C. -1), Government of India, New Delhi which is to oversee the implementation of national Common Minimum Programme (C.M.P.) of the United Progressive Alliance (U.P.A.) Government of India. The functions of the National Advisory Council (N.A.C.) include:

a)   To monitor the progress of the implementation of the Common Minimum Programme (C.M.P.).

b)   To provide inputs for the formulation of policy by the government and to provide support to the government in its legislative business.

As Member, N.A.C. Dr. Swaminadhan focused on **"Tribal Development"** among other things.

MEMBERSHIP OF PROFESSIONAL BODIES

Prof. Dr. D. Swaminadhan is a Member of reputed Professional Bodies like:

Fellow of Institution of Engineers (F.I.E.),

Fellow, Indian National Academy of Engineering (F.N.A.E.);

Fellow, Andhra Pradesh Academy of Sciences (F.A.P.A.S.);

Chartered Engineer (C.Eng);

Member, Indian Society for Technical Education (M.I.S.T.E.)

Member, Indian Science Congress Association (M.I.S.C.A.) and

Member, Indian Institute of Public Administration (I.I.P.A.), New Delhi.

AWARDS

1. **National Unity Award-'93'**, conferred for outstanding services, achievements and contributions, by the All India National Unity Conference, New Delhi

2. Honoured as an **'Eminent Scientist of India'** by the Andhra Pradesh Academy of Sciences, Hyderabad in September, 1993

3. **'Festival Award 93'** presented by the Delhi Telugu Academy, for his valuable contributions in the field of Planning

4. **'Vijaya Rattna Award'** presented by the International Friendship Society of India, New Delhi for enriching human life and outstanding contributions, February, 1994

5. **Rajiv Gandhi Excellence Award - 1993** presented by the Shiromani Institute, New Delhi August, 1994

6. **Manav Sewa Puraskar** presented by the Institute of Economic Studies, New Delhi June, 1995

7. **International Cultural Diploma of Honour**, awarded by the American Biographical Institute - 1995

8. **Awarded D.Sc., (Honoris Causa)** by the Dr. B.R. Ambedkar Open University, Hyderabad at its VIIth Convocation 23rd August, 1994

9. Awarded PhD (Honoris Causa) by Jawaharlal Nehru Technological University (J.N.T.U.),Hyderabad

10. Honoured and presented an Institution of Engineers' plaque for his eminence and outstanding contribution to the profession of engineering at the **Glimpses of Engineering Personalities** programme organised at the time of the Tenth Indian Engineering Congress held at Jaipur on December 20-23, 1995

11. On personal invitation **biographical entry** included in the **Dictionary of International Biography - Twenty Fifth Edition** scheduled for publication in January/February 1997 by the International Biographical Centre, England

12. Nominated as an **International Man of the year for 1996/97** by the International Bio-Graphical Centre, Cambridge, England

13. Nominated to 2000 outstanding people of 20th Century, International Biographical Centre, Cambridge, England

14. "Twentieth Century Award For Achievement" International Biographical Centre, Cambridge, England

15. "Sri Lankapally Bullayya Life Time Achievement Award", 2001

16. Rashtriya Vikas Shiromani Award–2005 for contribution in the field of Planning, awarded by Delhi Telugu Academy, New Delhi

17. The Leading Engineers of the World – 2007 award by the International Biographical Centre, Cambridge, England

18. Life Time Achievement Award – Sri Ramanuja Mission Trust, Chennai on 20th June, 2008

19. Life Time Achievement Award – Indian Society for Technical Education – Andhra Pradesh Chapter, Hyderabad December, 2008

20. 'Distinguished Indian' in recognition of his outstanding contribution to the Scientific community and his Life Time Achievement in the academic and Research and development presented by Board of Directors of Pentagram Research Centre, Hyderabad on 7th January, 2009

21. 'The Great Son of the Soil', in recognition of his outstanding services, achievements and contribution by All India Conference of Intellectuals, Andhra Pradesh Intellectuals Conference on 22nd February, 2009.

Committees Chaired

1. Chairman, A.I.C.T.E. High Power Committee on Mobilisation of Additional Resources for Technical and Management Education.

2. Chairman, Standing Committee on the Promotion and Coordination of Value Orientation of Education, constituted by the Ministry of Human Resource Development (H.R.D.), Government of India.

3. Chairman, Standing Committee on the Promotion and Coordination of University-Industry-National R&D Laboratories-Professional Bodies and National Academies Interaction, constituted by the Planning Commission.

4. Chairman, National Steering Committee of Technology Development Missions undertaken by the I.I.T.s and IISc., Bangalore, constituted by the Planning Commission.

5. Chaired UNESCO Forum on "Strategies for a University-Industry Cooperation Programme in Science, Technology and Engineering in India", organised by UNESCO at Delhi – January, 1996.

6. Convener (Chairman) of the U.G.C.'s Ninth plan visiting committees to (i) BITS, Pillani; (ii) Indian School of Mines (I.S.M.), Dhanbad; (iii) G.B.Pant University of Agriculture & Technology;

Committees Associated

1. Member-Secretary, U.G.C. High Power Standing Committee on utilising Electronic Media/Mass Communication.

2. Member-Secretary, U.G.C. Committee on T.V. Programmes on Teacher Education.

3. Member-Secretary, U.G.C. Expert Panel on Mass Communication.

4. Member-Secretary, T.V. Programme Committee set up by U.G.C.

5. Member-Secretary, U.G.C. Sixth Plan Review Committee of some Universities in South India.

6. Member-Secretary, Expert Committee set up by U.G.C. on Restructuring of Under-graduate courses at some of the colleges.

7. Member-Secretary, Expert Committee of the U.G.C. 6th Plan Visiting Committee to some of the Universities in the South.

8. Member-Secretary, Expert Committee on the Formulation of new Guidelines for M.Phil. Programmes in the Universities.

9. Member-Secretary, Expert Committee on Autonomous Colleges set up by U.G.C.

10. Member of the U.G.C. 7th Plan Visiting Committee to Bombay and S.N.D.T. Universities.

11. Member of the "Group on Satellite Services for Education" appointed by the Ministry of Human Resource Development, Government of India.

12. Member of the Governing Board and Academic Board of the Technical Teachers Training Institute, Madras.

13. Member of the Research Advisory Committee of the Department of Ocean Development.

14. Chairman of the Core Group on Value Orientation of Education set up by the Planning Commission.

15. Member-Secretary of the National Development Council Committee

    on Employment.

16. UGC Nominee on the Search Committee of Vice-Chancellor of Mohanlal Sukhadia University, Udaipur (Rajasthan) (July 2004).

17. UGC Nominee on the Search Committee for identification of Vice Chancellor of Sher-e-kashmir University of Agricultural Sciences and Technology, Jammu.

18. UGC Nominee on the Inspection Committee for Inspection of private universities in Chhattisgarh.

19. UGC Inspection Committee for inspecting Integral University, Lucknow (August, 2004).

20. Member of the Board of Governors of National Institute of Technology (N.I.T.), Himarpur.

21. Member, National Advisory Council (N.A.C.), Government of India, New Delhi.

22. Member, Panel on Pace of socio-economic change and development under the Constitution, **National Commission to Review the Working of the Constitution,** February 22, 2000

REPORTS PUBLISHED

1. Report of Core Group on Value orientation of Education, Planning Commission - October, 1992

2. Report of the High Power Committee on Mobilisation Resources for Technical Education, All India Council for Technical Education, New Delhi - March, 1994.

3. Draft Technology Policy for India, published by Dr. D. Swaminadhan Research Foundation [D.S.R.F.], Hyderabad-December, 1999.

BOOKS PUBLISHED

1. Book titled "Selected Speeches of Dr.D.Swaminadhan"-published by Patridge India-2013.

2. Book Titled " New world Government-Structure And Constitution" Published by Xlibist, Australia – 2019

3. Book titled " The Rise of a Tribal- An Autobiography" published by Book Trail Agency, USA.

4. Book titled " Unified Global Agenda and the World Government" published by Book Trail Agency, USA.

PAPERS PUBLISHED-NATIONAL

1. "A Model for University-Industry Symbiosis" Published in "University News" dated 14th May, 1990 of Association of Indian Universities.

2. Article on 'Higher Education and Human Development' for the Special Volume published at the 80th Annual Session of the Indian Science Congress Association held at Goa from 3rd to 6th January, 1993

3. Article titled "Making Higher Education More Purposeful" Published in the Republic Day, 1994 - Special Issue of Yojana.

4. Article titled "Distance Education Mode in Engineering and Technology" published in the book titled "New Horizons in Distance Education" edited by Prof. Bakhshish Singh, Consultant (Distance Education), U. G. C. – November, 1994.

5. Article titled "Ensuring Supply of Safe Drinking Water" published in the Republic Day 1995 Special Issue of Yojana dated 26.1.1995.

6. "Higher Education, Technical Education and Management Education: A Draft Approach paper for Ninth Plan". Included in the volume **"Knowledge Through our Life Time"** published by professor M.Madaiah Felicitation Committee, Mysore- 1997.

7. Article titled "Technical Education and Research in India - Need for Reorientation" published in the Journal University News Volume XXXIII dated 3.4.1995, brought out by the Association of Indian Universities, New Delhi.

8. As Chairman of the High Power Committee, published the Report of the High Power Committee on Mobilisation Resources for Technical Education, All India Council for Technical Education, New Delhi – March, 1994

9. D. Swaminadhan "Technology Capacity Building and Application for Sustainable Rural Development through Partnership Approach"

published in Journal of Rural Development. Vol.17 (3) pp. 407-419 (1998).

PAPERS PUBLISHED-INTERNATIONAL

1. Article titled Potentials for Universities, Industry and National Laboratories in India - The Inevitability of Closer Interaction published in the journal Industry & Higher Education (Vol. 7_No.) September 1993 issue published by In Print Publishing, U. K.

PAPERS PRESENTED-NATIONAL

1. Presented a research Paper on "Analysis of skew Articulated Cellular Bridge Decks" at the International Conference on "Bridges and Flyovers" organised by the Bureau of Industrial Consultancy and Research & Development, Jawaharlal Nehru Technological University, Hyderabad, February 8-10, 1991.

2. Presented a paper on "Distance Education Utilisation of I.N.S.A.T. Facility" at the National Seminar on "Challenge of Education - A Policy Perspective" with special reference to women's education, organised by the Montessory Mahila Kalasala, Vijayawada (A.P.) - 8th December, 1985.

3. 'Distance Education Mode in Engineering and Technology' at the Decennial International Seminar on Technical and Vocational Programmes through Distance Education organised by Dr. B.R. Ambedkar Open University, Hyderabad.

4. Contributed a paper on "I.N.S.A.T. for Distance Education in India" to the National Seminar on " Communications Technology as

applied to Education" held at Punjab University, Chandigarh, 5-7 November, 1986.

5. Presented a paper `Science Education and Quality of life' as one of the main Speakers at the Symposium in the 80th Annual Session of the Indian Science Congress Association Held at Goa from 3rd to 6th January, 1993.

6. Presented a paper on "Seeking for Excellence in Engineering, Technical and Management Education and Research in India" at the 81st Session of Indian Science Congress Association, held at Jaipur from 3rd-8th January, 1994.

7. Presentation at the 34th Annual Conference of the Indian Association for the Advancement of Medical Education on the topic "Multiprofessional Education and Quality of Life", held at Agra on 10.2.1995.

8. Paper on "Higher Education And Development" Presented at the Naional Seminar on "Fifty years of Development Experience – Retrospect and Prospect" organised by University of Mysore –18th-19th August 1997.

9. Presented a paper on "Technology Capacity Building and Application for the Development of Weaker Sections in Rural Areas" at the National Seminar on "Strategies for Socio-Economic and Political Development of Backward Classes" held at Hyderabad from 26th-27th November'1999.

10. Presented a paper on "Education Development of Backward Classes in India" at the National Seminar on "Strategies for Socio-Economic and Political Development of Backward Classes" held at Hyderabad from 26th-27th November'1999.

11. Presented a paper on "Education Development of Women in India" at the National Seminar on "Strategies for Socio-Economic and Political Development of Women" held at Hyderabad from 9th –10th June'2000

12. Presented a paper on "Economic Development of Minorities" at the National Seminar on "Strategies for Socio-Economic and Political Development of Minorities" held at Hyderabad from 7th –8th April'2000.

13. Presented a paper on "Women in Economic Development of India" at The National Seminar on "Strategies for Socio-Economic and Political Development of Women" held at Hyderabad from 9th –10th June'2000.

14. Presented a paper on "Culture of and Value Inculcation for National Reconstruction and world peace" at the National seminar on "value of Orientation of Education for National Reconstruction and World Peace" organised by the National Institute of Research and Social Action (NIRSA) Hyderabad form 30th –31st October'2000.

The following papers were presented at the National Conference on "University – Industry - R&D Organisations – Scientific Bodies Interaction and Co-operation: Policy perspectives"; Jointly organised by National Institute of Research and Social Action (NIRSA) and Osmania University College of Engineering (O.U.C.E.) during 11-12th August, 2001.

15. University – Industry Co-operation.

16. R&D Organisations – Industries Cooperation

17. Scientific Bodies and Engineering Associations and Academies: Their Partnership in the Cooperation.

18. International Experiences on University – Industry Partnership.

19. University – industry –R & D Labs Scientific and Engineering Academies/Bodies Co-operation: Policy Perspectives.

The following papers were presented at the National Conference on "Promotion of Communal Harmony: Strategies and Approaches", Jointly organised by Mahatma Gandhi International School of Research for Indian Freedom Movement and National Reconstruction (M.G.I.S.) and National Institute of Research and Social Action (NIRSA) during 9-10th November, 2001.

20. Communal Harmony and Spirit of Indian Freedom Movement.

21. Communal Harmony and Education.

22. Communal Harmony and Media.

23. Communal Harmony and Synthesis of Core Principles of Religions.

24. Communal Harmony and Political Parties.

25. Communal Harmony and the Constitutional Provisions.

The following papers were presented at the National Conference on "Children and Their Development in the Contemporary World: Strategies and Approaches"; organised by National Institute of Research and Social Action (NIRSA) and its Dr.B.R.Ambedkar Centre for Social Action during 8th-9th February, 2002.

26. "Children and their development in the Contemporary world: Children's education, Health and Nutrition"

27. "Children and their development in the Contemporary world: Media Role"

28. "Children and their development in the Contemporary world: Street Children, Child Labour, Child abuse and Children's Rights.

29. "Children and their development in the Contemporary world: Disabled Children"

30. "Children and their development in the Contemporary world: Orphaned Children due to Communal Riots, wars, terrorism and Calamities

31. "Children and their development in the Contemporary world: Girl child"

The following papers were presented at the National Conference on "Transforming India into a developed Nation: Harnessing Youth Power" jointly organised by Mahatma Gandhi National Institute of Research and Social Action (M.G.N.I.R.S.A.), Indian Institute of Chemical Technology(I.I.C.T.), National Geophysical Research Institute(NGRI) 25th – 26th October 2002.

32. "Transforming India into a Developed Nation: Need for Technology Superiority"

33. "Strengthening the Moral of the Country through Education in Human Values"

34. "Unity and Integrity of India and Role of Youth"

The following papers were presented at the National Conference on "Globalisation and Higher Education and Research in India: Need for Innovations" jointly organised by Mahatma Gandhi National Institute of Research and Social Action (MGNIRSA) and its Centre for Policy Research(C.P.R.), 13th – 15th February 2002.

35. Higher Education and Research: International Experiences in University- Industry Cooperation"

36. Higher Education and Research: Equity, Access, Relevance, Quality and Excellence"

37. Research Excellence in India: issues, Problems and Remedies"

38. Higher Education and Research: Resources"

39. Virtual School of Higher learning (V.S.H.L.) – An Initiative.

40. University – Industry – R&D Labs – Scientific and Engineering Academics/Bodies Cooperation: Policy Perspectives.

The following papers were presented at the National Conference on "Indian Democracy: Contemporary Threats and Challenges" jointly organised by Mahatma Gandhi National Institute of Research and Social Action (MGNIRSA) and its Dr.B.R.Ambedkar Centre for Social Action and India Watch Group(I.N.W.A.G.) during 22nd – 23rd August, 2003.

41. "Indian democracy: Contemporary Threats to Unity and Integrity"

42. "Erosion in Human Values – Threat to Indian Democracy"

43. "Indian Democracy and Social Empowerment"

The following papers were presented at the National Conference on "Education and Science & Technology: Social Empowerment " organised by Mahatma Gandhi National Institute of Research and Social Action (MGNIRSA) and its Centre for Policy Research(C.P.R.), 12th – 13th December 2003.

44. Education and Social Empowerment.

45. Education and Science and Technology: economic empowerment of the Socially Disabled

46. Social Empowerment of Women

47. Socially Disabled: Political Empowerment

48. Advances in Science and Technology: Social Infrastructure

49. Presented a Paper on **National Policy on Tribals** at the National Conference on **"Tribal Policy for India"**, 6-7th Jan' 06 organised by Mahatma Gandhi National Institute of Research and Social Action (MGNIRSA) and its Alluri Seetharamaraju Centre for Tribal Studies and Research.

50. Presented a Paper on Model Villages and Social Infrastructure at **National Seminar on "Model Village" on 3rd-4th November, 2006** organised by Dr.D.Swaminadhan Research Foundation (D.S.R.F.) and its Development Organisations Network (D.O.N.E.T.).

KEYNOTE ADDRESS-NATIONAL

1. Delivered the Key Note Address at the Seminar on "Autonomous Colleges" organised at Pragati Mahavidyalaya Degree College, Hyderabad, during March 20, 1988.

2. Offered keynote paper titled "A Model for University-Industry Symbiosis" at the "Workshop on Swaminadhan Model" organized by the National Institute of Research and Social Action (NIRSA) J.N.T. University, Hyderabad, 29th August, 1989.

3. Delivered Keynote address on "University-Industry Interaction-Sponsored Research" at the Seminar on "Quality and Excellence in Higher Education" organised by the Andhra Pradesh State Council

of Higher Education, Hyderabad at the time of the State Vice-Chancellors Conference, 6th September, 1989.

4. Key Note Address on ` Approach to Higher Education Development in India in Nineties' at the Silver Jubilee Celebrations of the Madurai Kamaraj University, Madurai, Tamil Nadu on 14th July, 1993.

5. Keynote Address at the Symposium on "Resource Crunch and Science Education" at 81st session of Indian Science Congress Association held at Jaipur on 6th January, 1994.

6. Key note address at the Workshop on "Hyderabad Master Plan 2011" sponsored by Hyderabad Urban Development Authority on 17.8.1994.

7. Key Note address at the National Meet to discuss 'Issues and Guidelines Pertaining to the State Finance Commissions' on 28.10.1994 at New Delhi.

8. Key Note Address at the Seminar on "Industry-Management Institution Interface" organised by the Department of Commerce & Business Management, Punjab University, Chandigarh on 26.11.1994

9. Key Note Address at the National Workshop on "Codes of Practice for R.C. Structures" at the J.N.T. University, Hyderabad on 28.7.95.

10. Key Note Address at the Inaugural Function of the National Seminar on "Planning and Management of Technical Education", Jawaharlal Nehru Technological University, Hyderabad on 19.8.1995

11. Key Note Address at the Seminar on "Rural Urban Interfacing for Sustainable Growth" at the 28th Engineer's Day Celebrations organised by the Institution of Engineers (India), Andhra Pradesh State Centre, Hyderabad on 15.9.1995.

12. Valedictory Address at the First World Sports Congress organised by the Indian Institute of Sport, New Delhi on 4th December, 1995.

13. Key Note Address at the XIV Annual Conference of the Indian Society for Probability and Statistics Organised by the Dept. of Statistics, Osmania University, Hyderabad on 18.12.1995.

14. Keynote Address at the National Seminar on "50 Years of Independence and Economic Development of Dalits in India" University of Hyderabad, March 1999.

15. Key Note address paper on "Human Resource Development" – Seminar on Vision 2020 of A.P., organised by F.A.P.C.C.I., Hyderabad – 21- 22nd November, 1997

16. Keynote address on "Recent Developments in Concrete and Concrete Structures" celebrates of Concrete function organised by Indian Concrete Institute, Andhra Pradesh Local Centre, Visakhapatnam on 7th September'2000.

17. Key Note Address at the Inaugural Function of the National Seminar on "Strategies for Sustained Socio-Economic and Political Development of Minorities" during 7th –8th April'2000

PRESIDENTIAL ADDRESS-NATIONAL

1. Presidential Address at the National Meet on "Housing Needs, Finance, Legislation and Policy "organised by the Socio Economic Research Foundation, New Delhi, September, 1991.

2. residential Address at the Valedictory Function of the seminar on Value Education organised by the Indian Council of Philosophical Research, New Delhi on 1.7.92

3. Presidential Address on "Life and Message of Swami Vivekananda" at the Ramakrishna Mission, New Delhi on 6th February, 1994.

4. Presidential Address at the 2nd Meeting of State Urban Development Strategy & Housing Development Programmes held on 15.7.1994 at New Delhi.

5. Presidential Address at the Inaugural as well as the valedictory sessions of the "National Seminar on Rural Technologies" organised by the National Institute of Research and Social Action (NIRSA) and the National Institute of Small Industry Extension Training (N.I.S.I.E.T.) Hyderabad – July 1997.

6. Presidential Address at the Inaugural as well as the Valedictory functions of the "National Seminar on Fifty years of Independence – Indian Ethos and Human Values: Retrospect and Prospect" jointly organised by the National Institute of Research and Social Action (NIRSA) and the National Institute of Small Industry Extension Training, (N.I.S.I.E.T.) Hyderabad – 16-18th October 1997.

7. Presidential Address at the Inaugural function of the "International Research Centre for Indian Freedom Movement and National Reconstruction (IRECIFMANAR)" organised by the National Institute of Research and Social Action (N.I.R.S.A.), Hyderabad – 24th November 1997

8. Presidential Address at the Inaugural Session of the National Seminar on "Strategies for Tribal Transformation and Development" organised by the National Institute of Research and Social Action (N.I.R.S.A.), Hyderabad 18-19th December 1998.

9. Presidential Address at the Inaugural Session of the National Seminar on "Strategies for Sustained Socio-Economic and Political Development of Dallies" organised by the National Institute of Research and Social Action (N.I.R.S.A.), Hyderabad 29-30th April 1999.

10. Presidential Address at the Inaugural Session "International Technology Convention'99" organised by Dr.D.Swaminadhan Research Foundation [D.S.R.F.] and Indian Institute of Chemical Technology (I.I.C.T.), Hyderabad 2nd –4th November' 1999.

11. Presidential Address at the Inaugural of the National Seminar on "Strategies for Sustained Socio-Economic and Political Development of Backward Classes" organised by the Dr.D.Swaminadhan Research Foundation [D.S.R.F.],Hyderabad during 26th –27th November 1999.

12. Presidential Address at the Inaugural Session on National Seminar on "Strategies for Sustained Socio-Economic and Political Development of Minorities" organised by the Dr.D.Swaminadhan Research Foundation [D.S.R.F.],Hyderabad 7th –8th April 2000.

13. Presidential Address at the Inaugural of the National Seminar on "Strategies for Sustained Socio-Economic and Political Development of Women" organised by the Dr.D.Swaminadhan Research Foundation [D.S.R.F.], Hyderabad 9th-10th June'2000.

14. Presidential Address at the Inaugural Session on National Seminar on " Culture of Peace and Value Inculcation for National reconstruction and World Peace" organised by the Dr.D.Swaminadhan Research Foundation [D.S.R.F.], Hyderabad during 30th-31st October 2000.

15. Presidential Address at the Inaugural and Valedictory Session of the International S.C.I. 2000 "Systemics cybernatics & Informatics on Advances in Information Technology" organised by the National Institute of Research and Social Action (N.I.R.S.A.)], Hyderabad during 17th December 2000.

16. Presidential addresses at the inaugural session on 15th June of the International Seminar on "Human Security at the Dawn of the New Millennium: Challenges and Perspectives"; Jointly organised by N.I.R.S.A. & N.I.S.I.E.T. during 15-16th June, 2001.

17. Presidential addresses at the valedictory session on 16th June of the International Seminar on "Human Security at the Dawn of the New Millennium: Challenges and Perspectives"; Jointly organised by N.I.R.S.A. & N.I.S.I.E.T. during 15-16th June, 2001.

18. Presidential addresses at the Inaugural session on 20th July of the Two day seminar on "Modern Trends in Biotechnology and Sustainable Rural Development" Jointly organised by National Institute of Research and Social Action (NIRSA) and nisiet during 20-21st July 2001.

19. Presidential addresses at the inaugural session on 11th August of the National Conference on "University - Industry - R&D Organisations - Scientific Bodies Interaction and Co-operation: Policy Perspectives", Jointly organised by National Institute of Research and Social Action (NIRSA) and Osmania University College of Engineering (O.U.C.E.) during 11-12th August,2001

20. Presidential addresses at the Valedictory session on 21st July of the Two day seminar on "Modern Trends in Biotechnology and Sustainable Rural Development" Jointly organised by National

Institute of Research and Social Action (NIRSA) and nisiet during 20-21ˢᵗ July 2001

21. Presidential addresses at the Valedictory session on 12ᵗʰ August of the National Conference on "University - Industry - R&D Organisations - Scientific Bodies Interaction and Co-operation: Policy Perspectives", Jointly organised by National Institute of Research and Social Action (NIRSA) and Osmania University College of Engineering (O.U.C.E.) during 11-12ᵗʰ August,2001

22. Presidential addresses at the Inaugural sessions on 9ᵗʰ November of the National Conference on "Promotion of Communal Harmony: Strategies and Approaches", Jointly organised by Mahatma Gandhi International School of Research for Indian Freedom Movement and National Reconstruction (M.G.I.S.) and National Institute of Research and Social Action (NIRSA) during 9-10ᵗʰ November, 2001.

23. Presidential addresses at the Valedictory session on 10ᵗʰ November of the National Conference on "Promotion of Communal Harmony: Strategies and Approaches", Jointly organised by Mahatma Gandhi International School of Research for Indian Freedom Movement and National Reconstruction (M.G.I.S.) and National Institute of Research and Social Action (NIRSA) during 9-10ᵗʰ November, 2001.

24. Presidential addresses at the Inaugural sessions on 25ᵗʰ October, 2002 of the National Conference on "Transforming India Into a Developed Nation: Harnessing Youth Power" the National Institute of Research and Social Action (N.I.R.S.A.), the Indian Institute of Chemical Technology (I.I.C.T.), Hyderabad, the National Geophysical Research Institute (NGRI) and I.N.W.A.G. are jointly organising the two-day National Conference during 25ᵗʰ – 26ᵗʰ October, 2002 at Hyderabad.

25. Presidential addresses at the Valedictory sessions on 26th October, 2002 of the National Conference on "Transforming India Into a Developed Nation: Harnessing Youth Power" the National Institute of Research and Social Action (N.I.R.S.A.), the Indian Institute of Chemical Technology (I.I.C.T.), Hyderabad, the National Geophysical Research Institute (NGRI) and I.N.W.A.G. are jointly organising the two-day National Conference during 25th – 26th October, 2002 at Hyderabad.

26. Presidential addresses at the Inaugural sessions on 13th February, 2003 of the National Conference on "Globalisation and Higher Education and Research in India: Need for Innovations" jointly organised by the Mahatma Gandhi National Institute of Research and Social Action (MGNIRSA) and the Centre for Policy Research (C.P.R.) during 25th – 26th October, 2002 at Hyderabad.

27. Presidential addresses at the Inaugural sessions on 22nd August, 2003 of the National Conference on "Indian Democracy: Contemporary Threats and Challenges" organised by the Mahatma Gandhi National Institute of Research and Social Action (MGNIRSA) of Dr.B.R.Ambedkar Centre for Social Action and India Watch Group(I.N.W.A.G.) during 22nd – 23rd August, 2003 at Hyderabad.

28. Presidential addresses at the Inaugural sessions on 12th December, 2003 of the National Conference on "Education and Science & Technology: Social Empowerment" organised by the Mahatma Gandhi National Institute of Research and Social Action (MGNIRSA) of Centre for Policy Research(C.P.R.) during 12th-13th December, 2003 at Hyderabad.

29. Presidential addresses at the Inaugural sessions on 19th November, 2004 on National Conference on "Role of Social Science Research in National Development" jointly organised by the Mahatma Gandhi National Institute of Research and Social Action (MGNIRSA) of Centre for Policy Research(C.P.R.), I.A.S.S.I. & I.M.I. during 19th – 20th November 2004.

30. Presidential addresses at the Valedictory Session on 20th November, 2004 on National Conference on "Role of Social Science Research in National Development" jointly organised by the Mahatma Gandhi National Institute of Research and Social Action (MGNIRSA) of Centre for Policy Research(C.P.R.), I.A.S.S.I. & I.M.I. during 19th – 20th November 2004.

31. Presidential addresses at the Inaugural Session **National Conference on** "Dr. Ambedkar's Vision: Relevance to Contemporary India", **28-29**[th] **December, 2005** organised by the Mahatma Gandhi National Institute of Research and Social Action (M.G.N.I.R.S.A.).

32. Presidential addresses at the Inaugural Session on **National Conference on** "Tribal Policy for India", **6-7**[th] **Jan' 06** organised by Mahatma Gandhi National Institute of Research and Social Action (MGNIRSA)

33. Presidential addresses at the Inaugural Session on **National Seminar on** "Gandhi's Vision: Contemporary Relevance", **27**[th] **& 28**[th] **January, 2006 organised by** Mahatma Gandhi National Institute of Research and Social Action (MGNIRSA)

34. Presidential addresses at the Inaugural Session **National Conference on** "Vedic Knowledge: Contemporary Relevance" **16**[th] – **18**[th] **June, 2005** jointly organised by the J.N.I.A.S. & I-SERVE.

35. Presidential addresses at the Inaugural Session on **National Conference on** "Empowerment of Women" **on 6**[th]**-7**[th] **March, 2006** organised by Mahatma Gandhi National Institute of Research and Social Action (M.G.N.I.R.S.A.).

36. Presidential addresses at the Inaugural Session on **National Seminar on** "Recent Advances in Biotechnology and Bioinformatics" **on 24**[th] **-25**[th] **July 2006** organised by Mahatma Gandhi National Institute of Research and Social Action (M.G.N.I.R.S.A.).

37. Presidential addresses at the Inaugural Session on **National Conference on** "Advances in Technology – Need for Global Ethics" **on 11**[th] **October, 2006** organised by M.G.N.I.R.S.A.

38. Presidential addresses at the Inaugural Session **on National Seminar on** "Model Village" **on 3**[rd]**-4**[th] **November, 2006** organised by M.G.N.I.R.S.A.

39. Presidential addresses at the Inaugural Session **on National Seminar on** "Indian Philosophy and the Gravitational Theory", **30**[th] **November 2006 organised by J.N.I.A.S.**

40. Presidential addresses at the Inaugural Session **on National Conference on** "Defence, War and Peace" **31**[st] **December, 2006 organised by J.N.I.A.S.**

41. Presidential addresses at the Inaugural Session **on National Conference on** "Empowerment of Dalit Women: Retrospect and Prospect", **during 14**[th] **February, 2007** organised by M.G.N.I.R.S.A.

42. Presidential addresses at the Inaugural Session **on National Conference on** "Empowerment of Dalit Women: Retrospect and Prospect", **during 14**[th] **February, 2007 organised by** Mahatma Gandhi National Institute of Research and Social Action (M.G.N.I.R.S.A.).

43. Presidential addresses at the Inaugural Session **on National Seminar on** "Global Peace and Harmony: Retrospect and Prospect" **during 13th-14th March 2007 organised by** Mahatma Gandhi National Institute of Research and Social Action (M.G.N.I.R.S.A.).

44. Presidential addresses at the Inaugural Session **on National Conference on** "Domestic Violence on Women: Causes & Remedies" **during 23rd-24th March, 2007 organised by** Mahatma Gandhi National Institute of Research and Social Action (M.G.N.I.R.S.A.).

45. Presidential addresses at the Inaugural Session **on National Seminar on** "Tribal Medicinal System: And Its Contemporary Relevance" **during 27th – 28th April, 2007 organised by** Mahatma Gandhi National Institute of Research and Social Action (M.G.N.I.R.S.A.).

46. National Conference on "Emerging Trends in the use of Information & Communication Technologies" 21st September, 2007.

47. National Seminar on "Problems of Nutrition: Among the Rich and Among the Poor" On 29th February to 1st March, 2008.

48. National Seminar on "Genome Analysis in the Post-Genomic era and its Relevance to Society" 26th-28th October, 2007.

49. National Conference on "Advances in Fermentation Technology" 9th-10th November, 2008

50. National Seminar on "Nonviolence: A Tool for Induced Change", 28th-29th January, 2008.

51. National Seminar on "Resource Management and Village Panchayats Experiences and Emerging Concerns" 28th – 29th November, 2008.

INAUGURAL ADDRESS-NATIONAL

1. Delivered the Inaugural Address at the "Media Seminar on Mental Handicap" at the Thakur Hari Prasad Institute of Research and Rehabilitation for the Mentally Handicapped, Hyderabad, January, 1991

2. Delivered the Inaugural Address at the National Conference on "Towards Excellence in Exports" organised by the Institute of Marketing & Management, New Delhi, January, 1991.

3. Inaugural Address at the All India Seminar on "Educational and Training Needs for Industrial Safety and Health Management" organised by the Institution of Engineers (India), A. P. State Centre and National Safety Council, July, 1991.

4. Inaugural Address at the Technical Workshop on "Eighth Five Year Plan Scenarios" with Specific reference to Urban and Regional Development, organised by the Institute of Town Planners, New Delhi, September, 1991.

5. Inaugural Address at the Seminar on "Planning in Nineties and Beyond" organised by the Prakasam Institute of Development Studies, Hyderabad held on 14.12.1991.

6. Inaugural Address at the 33rd National Convention of the Indian Institution of Industrial Engineering on "Industrial Engineering in the Management of Total Productivity" held at Jamshedpur in September, 1991.

7. Inaugural Address at the Fourth Annual Management Education Convention of the Association of Indian Management Schools, Jamshedpur on 20.8.1992.

8. Inaugural Address at the National Workshop on "Modalities for Planning Education and Training Inputs for ensuring availability of relevant Technical Manpower" organised by the Institute of Applied Manpower Research on 29.10.1992.

9. Inaugural Address at the 8th Annual Conference of the Indian Mathematical Society at Banaras Hindu University, Varanasi on 22.3.1993

10. Inaugural Address at the National Seminar on "Role of Central Government/State Governments/all India council for Technical Education/University Grants Commission/Universities/ Directorates of Technical Education in Technical Education" organised by the Indian Society for Technical Education as part of their silver Jubilee celebrations on 19.10.1992.

11. Inaugural Address at the Science Day Celebrations at the Avinashilingam Institute for Home Science and Higher Education for Women, Coimbatore on 26.3.1993.

12. Inaugural Address at the National Symposium on 'Managing our Metropolises: New Directions for 21st Century' organised by the School of Planning and Architecture, New Delhi on 29th March 1993.

13. Inaugural Address at the N.C.R. Convention on "Globalisation of Indian Economy - Role of Materials Management" held at New Delhi on 23.4.1993.

14. Inaugural address at the All India Meeting on State Urban Development Strategy held at New Delhi on 20.5.1993.

15. augural Address at the Conference on 'Problems and Prospects of Industrial Development in the National Capital Region' organised

by Federation of Indian Chambers of Commerce & Industry on 5.6.1993 held at Bhiwadi, Rajasthan.

16. Inaugural Address on the occasion of the Training Programme on Formulation and financing of Urban Water Supply Projects organised by Indian Institute of Public Administration, New Delhi on 29.9.1993.

17. Inaugural Address at the High Level policy Seminar on "Subsidy Issues in Urban Sector" organised by the Society for Development Studies, New Delhi on 17.11.1993.

18. Inaugural Address at the International Conference on "Rehabilitation, Renovation and Repairs of Structures 1994-95" organised by the Department of Civil Engineering, Andhra University, Visakhapatnam on 9th January 1994.

19. Inaugural Address at the International Symposium/Workshop on Boiling, Condensation and Two-Phase Flow Heat Transfer organised by the Department of Mechanical Engg., Andhra University, Visakhapatnam on 10th January 1994.

20. Inaugural Address at the National Seminar on The Role of Voluntary Agencies in Implementing the C.B.R. Approach for Mentally Handicapped and Mentally I11 at T. H. P. I., Hyderabad on 23rd April 1994.

21. Inaugural Address at the National Workshop on System Dynamics at the College of Engineering, Andhra University, Visakhapatnam on 9.5.1994.

22. Inaugural Address at the IInd National Conference on Increasing Access to Distance Education: An Agenda for Action at the S.V. University, Tirupati on 13.5.94.

23. Inaugural Address at the Golden Jubilee Seminar on "Computer Aided Engineering of Process Plants", organised by Indian Institute of Chemical Technology, Hyderabad on 16.11.1994.

24. Inaugural Address at the International Conference on "Engineering Education - An Indian Perspective" organised by the College of Engineering, Andhra University and Indian Society for Technical Education, A.U. Chapter at Visakhapatnam on 21.11.1994

25. Inaugural Address at the IInd International Conference on "Remote Sensing and G.I.S.- 'I.C.O.R.G. - 94'" organised by the Jawaharlal Nehru Technological University, Hyderabad on 3rd December, 1994.

26. Inaugural Address at the Policy Seminar on "Integrated Human Settlement Programme" organised by Society for Development Studies (S.D.S.) on December 8, 1994.

27. Inaugural Address at the Seminar on "Technology for a Better Tomorrow" at the 9 th Indian Engineering Congress organised by the Institution of Engineers (India) at Calcutta on 18.12.1994.

28. Inaugural Address at the National Conference on "Civil Engineering Materials and Structures" organised by the Department of Civil Engineering, University College of Engineering, Osmania University, Hyderabad on 19.1.1995.

29. Inaugural Address at the Two-Day Seminar on "Emerging New Social Order", organised by the Fulbright Alumni Association, Bangalore Chapter on 11.2.1995

30. Inaugural Address at the Twenty Fourth Orientation Programme for College and University Lecturers at the Academic Staff College, University of Mysore, Mysore on 12th June, 1995.

31. Inaugural Address at the Two Day Seminar on "Planning and Management of Technical Education in India" held at Punjab University, Chandigarh on 22.3.1995.

32. Inaugural Address at the Seminar on "Technologies for Educational Networking" organised by the Indira Gandhi National Open University, New Delhi on 1.11.1995.

33. Inaugural Address at the XIV Annual Conference of the Indian Society for Probability and Statistics organised by the Dept. of Statistics, Osmania University, Hyderabad on 18.12.1995

34. Inaugural Address at the Engineers' Day Seminar on "Engineering Manpower in India – The Challenges Ahead" organised by the Institution of Engineers (India), A.P. State Centre - 13th September 1997.

35. At the Workshop on "Law, Development & Information Technology Act – 2000: during 8th September'2000 jointly Organised by College of Engineering & Dr.B.R.Ambedkar College of law, Andhra University, Visakhapatnam.

VALEDICTORY ADDRESS –NATIONAL

1. Valedictory Address at the Fourth National Workshop on `Integrated Rural Energy Programme in Eighth Plan' organised by the Planning Commission and Government of Andhra Pradesh in March, 1992

2. Valedictory Address at the 35 th Technical Convention of the Institution of Electronics and Telecommunication Engineers, New Delhi on 6.9.1992.

3. Valedictory Address at the "National Conference on Entrepreneurship in the New Millennium: Challenges and Prospects" organised by the National Institute for Small Industry Extension Training [N.E.S.I.E.T.], Hyderabad on 9th January 2001.

4. Valedictory Address at the "National Conference on Entrepreneurship in the New Millennium: Challenges and Prospects" organised by the National Institute for Small Industry Extension Training [N.E.S.I.E.T.], Hyderabad on 9th January, 2001.

ENDOWMENT LECTURERS/SPEECHES/TALKS-NATIONAL

1. Delivered an Extension Lecture on "Modern Electronic Computers in Science & Engineering" at A.V. College of Arts and Science, Hyderabad, March, 1980

2. Lecture on "Role of Sri Sathya Sai Education in 21st Century" at the Sri Sathya Sai Institute of Higher Learning, Prasanthinilayam, Puttaparthi on 20th November, 1993

3. Delivered the Silver Jubilee Memorial Lecture " A Perspective Towards Challenges on Science and Technology for Rural India" at Pravara Rural Engineering College, Loni (Maharashtra) I.N.D.I.A., March 1, 1990.

4. Lecture on "Changed Economic Scenario - Imperatives for Higher Education in India" at the Mysore University, Mysore on 25.11.1993.

5. Sri Rebala Lakshminarasa Reddy Endowment Lecture on "Imperatives of University-Industry-R & D Organisation Interaction for National Development" at Sri Venkateswara University, Tirupati in February, 1992.

6. Delivered the Late Sri Damodaram Sanjeevaiah Endowment Lecture on "Reforms in Higher Education & Research in India" at Sri Venkateswara University, Tirupati on 12th April, 1995.

7. Foundation Day Lecture titled "Technological Superiority _ Pre-Requisite for Economic Survival in the Changed Global Scenario" at the Central Building Research Institute (C.B.R.I.), Roorkee on 10.2.1996.

8. Delivered a talk on what holds the University and the Industry?" at Engineers Meet organised by the Institution of Engineers (India), Kakinada paper Centre, Kakinada, 23rd February, 1989.

9. Andhra Bank Endowment Lecture on "India's Planning in Nineties" at Andhra University, Visakhapatnam in March, 1992.

10. A.B. Shetty Memorial Endowment Lecture on "Planning for Rural Development" at Mangalore University, Mangalore on 12th March, 1993.

11. Lecture at the National Seminar on Science and Technology-Development and Priorities organised by the Andhra Pradesh Academy of Sciences, Hyderabad on 12th September, 1993. `Changed Economic Scenario-Need for Approach Reorientation Towards Education and Research in Science and Technology in India.'

12. Lecture at the Himachal Pradesh University, Shimla on " Challenges to Higher Education and Research in India" on 11.10.1994.

13. Delivered the 7th Dr. A.N. Khosla Memorial Lecture on "Technical Education and Research in India – Need for Reorientation" at the 9th Indian Engineering Congress organised by the Institution of Engineers (India) at Calcutta on 18.12.1994

14. Extra Mural Lecture titled "Changing Times – Inevitability of Universities' Reorientation" at the Roorkee University, Roorkee on 9.2.1996.

15. Resource Lecturer on "Technological Development – Pre-requisite for Economic Superiority" delivered at Andhra University, Visakhapatnam on 8th September'2000

ADDRESSES AT VARIOUS FORUMS-NATIONAL

1. Address delivered as a Guest of Honour at the National Seminar on Rural Sanitation Held at New Delhi on 16.9.1992.

2. Address at the Expert Group Meeting to Deliberate on Implications of Economic Reforms for the Urban Sector organised by the Planning Commission on 17th March, 1993.

3. Address as the Chief Speaker on the panel of Gandhi and Value Education" in the XVI Annual Conference of the Indian Society of Gandhian Studies at the Jain Vishva Bharati Institute, Ladnun on 12th December, 1993.

4. Address at the Inaugural Function of the 68th Annual Meeting of the Association of Indian Universities on 18.12.93 at the University of Delhi

5. Address as a Guest of Honour on the occasion of World and Environment – Breaking the Vicious Circle' organised by the world Institution Building Programme at New Delhi on 5.6.1993.

6. Address at the Inaugural Function of 1993 World Environment Congress on 22-24 December, 1993

7. Address at the Conference of International Friendship Society of India on "Economic Growth & National Integration" at New Delhi on 3rd February, 1994.

8. Address as a Guest of Honour at the Inaugural Function of the U.G.C. Sponsored National Symposium and Workshop on Environmental Education in University Curricula organised by A.P. State Council for Higher Education at J. N. T. University, Hyderabad on 21.3.1994

9. Address at the A.I.U. Seminar on Accountability in Higher Education at University of Poona, Pune, on 12.11.1994.

10. Address at the Conference of Vice-Chancellors on Accreditation and Assessment Council - System and Modus Operandi at University of Poona, Pune, on 13.11.1994.

11. Address at the Seminar in the International Conference on "Engineering Education - An Indian Perspective" organised by the College of Engineering, Andhra University and Indian Society for Technical Education A.U. Chapter at Visakhapatnam on 21.11.1994.

12. Address as a Special Guest of Honour at the 15th India-NRI World Convention organised by the N.R.I. Institute at New Delhi on December 22, 1994.

13. Address at the Valedictory Session of the Second National Children's Science Congress organised by the NCSTC-Network at New Delhi on December 31, 1994.

14. Address on the topic "Making Engineering Education relevant to Industry" at the Indo- British Seminar on "Industry- Institute Interaction" held at New Delhi on 6.3.1995.

15. Address at the Seminar on Housing and Urban Development organised by the Institute of Economic Studies, New Delhi on 30th June, 1995.

16. Address at the Valedictory Function of the 30th International Training Programme on Manpower Planning" organised by the Institute of Manpower Research, New Delhi on 26th October, 1995.

17. Address at the Platinum Jubilee Celebrations of the Institution of Engineers (India) at Cochin on 9.12.1995.

18. Address at the UNESCO Forum on"Strategies for University Industry Cooperation in Engineering, Sciences and Technology in India" organised by UNESCO at New Delhi on 19.1.1996.

19. Address at the Workshop on "Rural Higher Education" organised by

20. the National Council of Rural Institutes, Hyderabad on 2.3.1996.

CONVOCATION ADDRESSES-NATIONAL

1. Convocation Address at the 15th Convocation of the Institute of Medical Sciences, Banaras Hindu University, Varanasi on 10.4.1993.

2. Convocation Address at the 12th Convocation of Dayalbagh Educational Institute, Agra on 28th January, 1994.

3. Convocation Address at the 12th Convocation of the Dayalbagh Educational Institute, Agra on " Higher and Technical Education in India" published in the University News, Volume XXXII, No. 18 dated 2.5.1994 by the Association of Indian Universities, New Delhi.

4. Convocation Address at the Golden Jubilee Convocation of the D. A. V. (P.G.) College, Dehradun on 22.4.1996.

PAPERS PRESENTED-INTERNATIONAL

1. Research paper on "A new method for the analysis of Articulated Cellular Bridge Decks" Presented at the Fourth Australian Conference on "The Mechanics of Structure and Materials " University of Queens land, Brisbane, Australia, August,1973.

2. Presented a paper on "Utilisation of I.N.S.A.T. Facility for Higher Education in India" at the International Conference on "New Technologies in Higher Education" held at Delhi during November 28-29, 1985 on the occasion of the Golden Jubilee Celebrations of the Association of Indian Universities.

3. Presented a paper titled "Utilisation of INSAT-1B for Higher Education" at the seminar on the Role of Higher Education in Developing Countries, organised by the United States Educational Foundation in India, New Delhi on January 15, 1985.

4. Co-author of the paper on "open Higher Education through Distance Teaching" Presented at the 2nd International Conference on "open Higher Education: Innovations and Technology" organized by Ramkhamhaeng University, Bangkok, March 24-28, 1987.

5. "University-Industry-Engineer Partnership for Sustainable Development" by Dr.D.Swaminadhan, Member, Planning Commission, G.O.I.Paper sent for presentation at the World Congress of Engineering Education and Industry leaders, Paris, July 1996.

6. "Inevitability of University-Industry Cooperation in R&D for India" Dr.D.Swaminadhan, Member, Planning Commission, G.O.I Paper sent for presentation at the World Congress of Engineering Education and Industry leaders, Paris, July 1996.

The following papers were presented at International seminar on "Human Security At The Dawn of the New Millennium: Challenges And Perspectives", during 15-16th June, 2001, Jointly organised by N.I.R.S.A. and N.I.S.I.E.T.:

7. World Peace and Human Security

8. Development and Human Security

9. State Ideologies and Human Security

10. Human Rights and Human Security

11. Environment and Human Security

12. Advances in Science and Technology and Human Security.

Keynote Address-National

1. Delivered the Key Note Address at the Seminar on "Autonomous Colleges" organised at Pragati Mahavidyalaya Degree College, Hyderabad, during March 20, 1988.

2. Offered keynote paper titled "A Model for University-Industry Symbiosis" at the "Workshop on Swaminadhan Model" organized by the National Institute of Research and Social Action (NIRSA) J.N.T.University, Hyderabad, 29th August, 1989.

3. Delivered Keynote address on "University-Industry Interaction – Sponsored Research" at the Seminar on "Quality and Excellence in Higher Education" organised by the Andhra Pradesh State Council of Higher Education, Hyderabad at the time of the State Vice-Chancellors Conference, September, 1989.

4. Key Note Address on ` Approach to Higher Education Development in India in Nineties' at the Silver Jubilee Celebrations of the Madurai Kamaraj University, Madurai, Tamil Nadu on 14th July, 1993.

5. Keynote Address at the Symposium on "Resource Crunch and Science " at 81st session of Indian Science Congress Association held At Jaipur on 6th January, 1994.

6. Key note address at the Workshop on "Hyderabad Master Plan 2011" sponsored by Hyderabad Urban Development Authority on 17.8.1994

7. Key Note address at the National Meet to discuss 'Issues and Guidelines Pertaining to the State Finance Commissions' on 28.10.1994 at New Delhi

8. Key Note Address at the Seminar on "Industry-Management Institution Interface" organised by the Department of Commerce & Business Management, Punjab University, Chandigarh on 26.11.1994

9. Key Note Address at the National Workshop on "Codes of Practice for R.C. Structures" at the J.N.T. University, Hyderabad on 28.7.95.

10. Key Note Address at the Inaugural Function of the National Seminar On "Planning and Management of Technical Education", Jawaharlal Nehru Technological University, Hyderabad on 19.8.1995

11. Key Note Address at the Seminar on "Rural Urban Interfacing for Sustainable Growth" at the 28th Engineer's Day Celebrations organised by the Institution of Engineers (India), Andhra Pradesh State Centre, Hyderabad on 15.9.1995

12. Valedictory Address at the First World Sports Congress organised by The Indian Institute of Sport, New Delhi on 4th December, 1995.

13. Key Note Address at the XIV Annual Conference of the Indian Society Probability and Statistics Organised by the Dept. of Statistics,Osmania University, Hyderabad on 18.12.1995

14. Keynote Address at the National Seminar on "50 Years of Independence and Economic Development of Dalits in India" University of Hyderabad, March 1999.

15. Key Note address paper on "Human Resource Development" – Seminar on Vision 2020 of A.P., organised by F.A.P.C.C.I., Hyderabad - 21- 22nd November,1997.

16. Keynote address on "Recent Developments in Concrete and Concrete Structures" organised by Indian Concrete Institute, Andhra Pradesh Local Centre, Visakhapatnam on 7th September'2000.

17. Key Note Address at the Inaugural Function of the National Seminar on "Strategies for Sustained Socio-Economic and Political Development of Minorities"during –8th April'2000

KEYNOTE ADDRESS-INTERNATIONAL

Key Note Address at the Inaugural Conference of Commonwealth Engineers' Council 50th Anniversary on "The Engineer's Contribution to Sustainability" at London on 19.3.1996

WORLD INTELLECTUAL FORUM (WIF)

Prof. Dr. D. Swaminadhan Research Foundation (DSRF), Hyderabad, India, which is a registered Society and Sri Ramanuja Mission Trust (SRMT), Chennai, India took the initiative in mooting the idea of the Independent Global Watch Approach and established the WORLD INTELLECTUAL FORUM (WIF) at Hyderabad, India. The World Intellectual Forum is a new initiative aimed at awakening the powers of the mind, consciousness, awareness, spiritual intelligence, intellect, reason, scientific expertise, academic excellence, and human creativity and genius to try to tackle collectively and cooperatively the most pressing problems facing the planet.

Prof.Dr. D. Swaminadhan is the Global Chair for the WIF.

THE NEW WORLD GOVERNMENT

The present system of world Governance proves to be wanting in tackling complex world problems. The point in case is that of the United Nations Organization (UNO). The United Nations Organization was created in 1945 with the objective "to save succeeding generations from the scourge of war". However, war preparations and wars have continued. All the disarmament conventions, commissions, studies and resolutions of the U.N. have failed to stop the increase and spread of military arms for war; have failed to stop the introduction of new technologies for more destructive weapons; have failed to stop more nations from acquiring nuclear weapons and have failed to achieve disarmament. The UN has no authority or jurisdiction to end the wars, there is need for seeking innovative approaches for forming a New World Government System as an alternative to UNO. Even great Statesmen and philosophers like Jawaharlal Nehru, Sarvepalli Radhakrishnan, Albert Einstein, Bertrand Russell, Jan Tinbergen, Ban Ki-moon, John F. Kennedy, Mikhail Gorbachev, Pope Benedict XVI, and Winston Churchill - all in one way or the other advocated the need for a World Government.

The Author proposed for the formation of a New World Government (as the Global Chair, World Intellectual Forum (WIF), Hyderabad) and suggested the Structure and Constitution for a New Democratic, Federal and Presidential form World Government as an alternative to UNO

UNIFIED GLOBAL AGENDA

WORLD SPACE COUNCIL

Space exploration and cooperation is an important issue in the context of future habitational needs to settle on Mars and other Planets. Space race among countries is on the increase which may lead to domination of one country over the other in the space. Apart from this, there may be a possibility of Planet wars involving Earth Planet. Therefore, Earth Citizens should be prepared for such a situation. In view of such a contingency, the New World Government establishes the WORLD SPACE COUNCIL (WSC) for coordination and cooperation among Nations in Space Exploration and to discourage domination of any nation. The Council consists of countries in space exploration, presently 70 countries, as Members.

GLOBAL SPACE RESEARCH INSTITUTE (GSRI)

The Council creates a space research Institute called "Global Space Research Institute (GSRI)". This Institute not only takes the lead in Space Research but also NETWORK all the Space Research Institutes and Centres. It will be governed by the World Space Council as its General Council(GC) and an Executive Board(EB) of Experts appointed by the General Council to act as an Executive Body.

REFERENCES

1. D. Swaminadhan, Proposal for Formation of the New Federal WorldGovernment. https://drive.google.com/file/d/15mrLdjos4vp5t bcdeuhtYEkStQzMWN_5/view?usp=sharing

2. The Constitution of India.

3. Prof.Dr.D.Swaminadhan," The New World Government-Structure And Constitution" Published by Xlibris Publishers, Australia.

4. Tthe Wikipedia, the free encyclopedia

5. "The Rise of a Tribal- An Autobiography," Published by Book Trail Agency, Cansas City, USA.

6. Source: Ministry of Environment, NITI Aayog, Ministry of Health, Press Information Bureau, Census of India, Ministry of External Affairs, Union Budget, Reserve Bank of India.

7. Vikaspedia portal, IndiaDevelopmentGateway(InDG),initiative Centre for Development of Advanced Computing (C-DAC)

8. Report of the National Commission to Review of the Working Of Constitution, 2002.

9. Tenth Five year Plan 2002-2007, Planning Commission, Govt. of India.

10. National Policy on Education (NPE) and Programme of Action (POA), 1992, Government of India.

11. National Seminar on 'Strategies for Tribal Transformation and Development' organised by National Institute of Research and Social Action(NIRSA) during 18-19th December 1998 in collaboration with the National Institute of Small Industries Extension Training (NISIET), Yousufguda, Hyderabad.

12. National Seminar on 'Strategies for Sustained Socio-Economic and Political Development of Dalits' organised by National Institute of Research and Social Action(NIRSA) during 29th-30th April 1999.

13. National Seminar on 'Strategies for Sustained Socio- Economic and Political Development of Backward Classes' organised by National Institute of Research and Social Action (NIRSA) during 26th-27th November 1999.

14. National Seminar on 'Strategies for Socio-Economic and Political Development of Minorities' organised by National Institute of Research and Social Action (NIRSA) during 7th-8th April'2000.

15. National Conference on "Children and their Development in the Contemporary World: Strategies and Approaches" organised by National Institute of Research and Social Action (NIRSA) during 8th-9th February, 2002, Hyderabad.

16. National Seminar on 'Strategies for Socio-Economic and Political Development of Women' organised by National Seminar on 'Strategies for Socio-Economic and Political Development of Women' organised during 9th-10h June '2000.

17. A Consultation paper on "Pace of Socio-Economic change under the Constitution" by the National Commission to Review the Working of the Constitution, on May, 2001, New Delhi.

18. National Seminar on 'Strategies for Tribal Transformation and Development' organised by National Institute of Research and Social Action(NIRSA) during 18-19th December 1998 in collaboration with the National Institute of Small Industries Extension Training (NISIET), Yousufguda, Hyderabad.

19. National Seminar on 'Strategies for Sustained Socio-Economic and Political Development of Dalits' organised by National Institute of Research and Social Action(NIRSA) during 29th-30th April 1999.

20. National Seminar on 'Strategies for Sustained Socio-Economic and Political Development of Backward Classes' organised by National Institute of Research and Social Action (NIRSA) during 26th-27th November 1999.

21. National Seminar on 'Strategies for Socio-Economic and Political Development of Minorities' organised by National Institute of Research and Social Action (NIRSA) during 7th-8th April'2000.

22. National Seminar on 'Strategies for Socio-Economic and Political Development of Women' organised by National Seminar on 'Strategies for Socio-Economic and Political Development of Women' organised during 9th-10th June '2000.

23. Report of the Working Group for Empowering the Scheduled Tribes during the Tenth Five Year Plan (2002-2007) – Ministry of Tribal Affairs, Govt. of India, New Delhi.

24. Tenth Five Year Plan (2002 – 2007) Volume II, Planning Commission, Govt. of India, New Delhi.

25. Consultation Paper on Pace of Socio-Economic change under the Constitution, National Commission to Review the Working of the Constitution (May 2001), Govt. of India, New Delhi

26. National Seminar on "Strategies for Tribal Transformation and Development" 18-19th December, 1998 organised by National Institute of Research and Social Action, Hyderabad.

27. Discussion in the National Advisory Council (NAC), Govt. of India, New Delhi.

28. Report of the National Commission to Review of the Working of the Constitution, 2002.